M000022211

Healed His Way

LEARNING TO TRUST THE GREAT PHYSICIAN

WELLNESS COACH & HEALING MINISTER

Chelsie Ward BSN, RN

Foreword by Robert Rakowski, DC, CCN, DACBN, DIBAK

HEALED HIS WAY: Learning to Trust the Great Physician

© 2018 Chelsie Ward.

All rights reserved. No part of this publication may be reproduced, distributed, or transmitted in any form or by any means, including photocopying, recording, or other electronic or mechanical methods, without the prior written permission of the publisher, except in the case of brief quotations embodied in critical reviews and certain other noncommercial uses permitted by copyright law. For permission requests, please contact the author.

ISBN (Print Edition): 978-1-7323715-0-7

ISBN (Kindle Version): 978-1-7323715-1-4

Library of Congress Control Number (LCCN): 2018906011

Printed in the United States of America

Published by Chelsie Ward, Dickinson, TX | www.chelsieward.com

Prepared for publication by Wendy K. Walters | www.palmtreeproductions.com

DISCLAIMER: No statements in this book are intended to diagnose, treat, cure, or prevent any disease. The recommendations found herein are based on the personal research and experiences of the author. You should consult your physician before trying any supplements, nutrition or diet regimen.

Unless otherwise noted, Scripture has been taken from The Holy Bible, Berean Study Bible (BSB). Copyright© 2016 by Bible Hub. Used by permission. All rights reserved worldwide.

To contact the author: www.chelsieward.com

PRAISE FOR HEALED HIS WAY

The modern world's constant demand for instant solutions and immediate gratification has led us to a national health crisis. Our food does not have the nutrients we need to sustain our immune systems and the constant reliance on pills for the temporary relief of the symptoms brought on by processed foods and unhealthy lifestyles has prevented us from achieving long term health.

We need voices who can lead us away from unhealthy practices to a lifestyle that once again embraces what is best for us. Fortunately, God is raising up people who can point the way back from over processed, chemical laden "foods" and inappropriately prescribed drugs to the health focused foods and life choices that build up our immune systems and strengthen our bodies. Chelsie Ward is one of these people and her book, *Healed His Way,* is a brilliant work on getting healthy and staying strong. She shares her own journey through sickness, and medications wrongly applied, to finding long term vitality and joy.

This book needs to be in every home because we are all being affected by these issues and we all need to find real solutions, not temporary ones. Read this book and practice what Chelsie Ward teaches and your body will respond with a level of energy and vitality you did not believe was possible.

—JOAN HUNTER
Author/Healing Evangelist
www.joanhunter.org

I am honored to know Chelsie Ward as a dear friend, healing minister, prayer intercessor, and nutritional consultant in my life. The first time I met Chelsie, I felt and saw her passion for Jesus, health, healing, and wholeness—God's way! She models optimal health in the way she lives.

Chelsie is transparent, raw, and real which unlocks major breakthrough. God has not only healed Chelsie, but has given her countless tools and strategies for your success!

Chelsie has taken us inside her personal journey in an extremely transparent way, accompanied by her studies to write *Healed His Way*. This is the most comprehensive book I've ever read in regards to health. It covers topics you didn't even know you wanted to learn about!

She courageously holds nothing back in sharing her struggles and how Jesus helped her overcome her own health challenges. As you read, I urge you to write down what the Holy Spirit speaks to you regarding the wisdom He has given Chelsie. God will honor your stewardship of His revelation and counsel. It's no mistake you are reading this book. I know it contains keys just for YOU!

I am a huge fan of Chelsie Ward, and this book rocked my world! Chelsie is a forerunner and pioneer for Jesus advancing the truth of God's word through healing the body and soul ... *Healed His Way!*

—HILARY LYNNE
Evangelist/Speaker
Founder of His Love Empowers Miracles
www.HLEMinistries.com

I have known Chelsie for several years. She is not only my role model, but also my subject matter expert when it comes to clean eating and healthy living. I'm excited that she put her real-life experiences and lessons into this book so that all who read it can reap the benefits.

This book will enlighten and educate you on the many facets of being healed God's way. It will encourage you to make changes in your own life if you need healing, or just want to improve your lifestyle. Chelsie gives you the knowledge, resources, and tools to make the transition from unhealthy and sick, to healthy, healed, and free.

Healed His Way came straight from Chelsie's heart. Her transparency about her own life and struggles with wellness prove she is authentic and genuine. I can tell you she is the Real Thing! She lives what she has written in this book daily, and as a result, is a beautiful person inside and out—spirit, soul, and body.

—EDIE ALLEN
Director of Crossroads Healing Rooms

As someone who has struggled to find a solution between the cause and the cure, I greatly appreciate Chelsie's encouragement to identify the root cause of the issue and focus on finding the healthiest way to function at optimal levels. How Chelsie has shared her healing process should remind all of us that our bodies were designed by the greatest Creator. It was with His design that He intended our smart bodies to heal themselves. I love Chelsie's candor as she shares her own journey to a more fulfilling life and I appreciate the challenge to "expect more for your future health."

—MELODY BARKER
Author, Speaker and Coach
www.melodybarker.com

Are you tired of having no energy, being sick, or experiencing chronic pain? Get *Healed His Way*, NOW! Chelsie addresses top causes of the American health breakdown and shares simple, yet life-changing solutions you can implement today. From perspiration to inflammation, Chelsie guides you through her "to-do" list for optimal health and wholeness.

—CHARITY BRADSHAW
Author, Writing & Publishing Coach
www.charitybradshaw.com

Written from a place of passion and expertise, *Healed His Way* is a breath of hope for those suffering from maladies for which modern, Western medicine has focused on alleviating symptoms rather than addressing and eliminating root causes. Chelsie's careful research and experience as a nurse makes her material trustworthy. Her own testimony provides credibility for her health choices, and her clear communication style makes her material approachable.

It was my great privilege to guide Chelsie through the publishing process for this book. I can attest to her painstaking process of checking facts, confirming information, and working tirelessly to make sure readers had the best, most accurate information possible. Unlike many books on healthy lifestyles, reading *Healed His Way* will not leave you feeling guilty about all the bad choices you have made in the past, nor overwhelmed that correcting them is impossible for an average person with a full-time load of family, work, and community commitments. Chelsie offers you bite-sized revelation that when applied <u>will</u> make a difference. Whether you can adapt to just one new healthy practice or bundle several together, you will see positive results to your energy, vitality, and overall wellness.

—WENDY K. WALTERS
Motivational Speaker, Branding & Publishing Expert
Director of The Favor Foundation
www.wendykwalters.com

CONTENTS

"By cleansing your body on a regular basis and eliminating as many toxins as possible from your environment, your body can begin to heal itself, prevent disease, and become stronger and more resilient than you ever dreamed possible!"

DR. EDWARD GROUP III

FOREWORD

by Robert Rakowski
DC, CCN, DACBN, DIBAK

It's been said that all wisdom is timeless, but that every generation needs a new voice. For many, Chelsie Ward is that new voice. In *Healed His Way*, Chelsie shares a spiritually-based, scientifically-sound, common-sense plan for maximizing your health. Chelsie pulls no punches as she calls out the enemy for intoxicating our air, water, and food. She also strongly encourages all of us to investigate every medical recommendation as if our life depended upon it.

Whereas she recognizes and acknowledges that God gave man the skill to create medicines, she clearly points out that as a society we tend to put an unhealthy trust in this creation of man. She clearly states "Unfortunately, there's a pill for everything now. It saddens me to know that at the time of this writing, the third leading cause of death is medical error, yet we tend to trust modern medicine more than we do God's medicine." In 571 BC, the Prophet Ezekiel wrote that the Lord created medicines out of the earth and that their leaves are to be used for healing (Ezekiel 47:12). Chelsie tells her own powerful story of how "normal" food and healthcare choices led to a spiraling path of decline. She shares how she sought wisdom and understanding from God and his servants to regain her vibrant health. She shares her story and God's treasures in a captivating and easy to read style. I highly recommend this book as a comprehensive guide to mental, physical, and most importantly—spiritual health.

On a more personal note, I have had the incredible joy of working with Chelsie and watching her incredible transformation. She is a shining light for all who have the joy of interacting with her. I trust that as you apply these timeless principles you will progress toward the life of abundance that we all deserve. Enjoy every step of your magnificent journey!

—ROBERT RAKOWSKI, DC, CCN, DACBN, DIBAK

Chiropractor, Kinesiologist, Certified Clinical Nutritionist,
Certified Biological Terrain Instructor,
Clinic Director of The Natural Medicine Center in Houston, TX
www.TheDrBob.com

Robert A. Rakowski, DC, CCN, DACBN, DIBAK is a Chiropractor, Kinesiologist, Certified Clinical Nutritionist, Certified Biological Terrain Instructor, and the clinic director of the Natural Medicine Center in Houston Texas. In addition to running a busy practice, Dr. Rakowski has lectured internationally for over 24 years on various topics in Natural and Lifestyle Medicine.

He has appeared on numerous television programs and international radio talk shows. He is a recognized expert in functional endocrinology and in-office diagnostic procedures to assess nutrition status. His clinical experience ranges from treating elite professional athletes to critically ill patients with a variety of cancers and autoimmune diseases.

INTRODUCTION

This is the story of my personal healing journey. There are many things God revealed to show me how to bring healing to my own body using what He has provided on this earth. There are also things He taught me that (thankfully) I did not have to experience to learn. I have included some of these as well because I know many need this information to restore or to walk in health. My goal is that as you read this, you will gain a basic understanding of the necessities for experiencing whole body healing the way God intended. Much of the book deals with physical healing, but understand that as we get to the root of illness, this also encompasses the soul as well as spiritual aspects.

I never thought I would tell this story, but my path to wellness has given me such a passion for seeing others well that I cannot keep my journey quiet any longer. I never imagined that the painful experience of being sick would uncover my destiny to bring healing to others. What the enemy intended to use to harm me, God has used to give me a story of His healing wonders. I pray that as you hear my story unfold, you will begin your own healing journey.

My testimony is meant to encourage you. As we discuss some of the things I experienced personally, I will share information that years of Holy Spirit guidance has taught me. Clinging to my Heavenly Father for wisdom has been my saving grace at times, and I am thrilled He has given me the opportunity to share it with you.

COMPLETE HEALING IS POSSIBLE WHEN THE BASIC BUILDING BLOCKS ARE PRESENT FOR A HEALTHY IMMUNE SYSTEM

I am truly passionate about you and your loved ones becoming well, having energy, ridding yourself of disease, and not having to worry about simple things like the flu or the common cold, or other scary diseases that many wrongfully accept as a normal part of the aging process. Complete healing is possible when the basic building blocks are present for a healthy immune system. I see my old, energy-depleted self of the past in many people I'm surrounded by on a daily basis. It saddens me that people are so sick and tired, and much of it can be blamed on our food system that's filled with confusing labels and flat out lies to get consumers to spend money on products that only make us sick, overweight, and fill our bodies with disease. You can heal your body from the inside out. It's not your fault you are sick. Our food system and environment have been attacked by the enemy. Our minds have also been attacked. We have become the victim on his playground.

There's a common mistake I see many people make when starting a journey to better choices for a healthier lifestyle. It's an all or nothing attitude. Many people try diet after diet only to fail because they feel it's too hard, or it stops working. They yo-yo up and down on the scale and their symptoms of sickness wax and wane as they try the latest fad diet and decide, "It's just not worth it ... I give up ... I will be sick, overweight, and exhausted forever." The weight continues to increase and the disease starts to become worse. They take a monthly trip to the pharmacy to fill their cabinets and bodies with things they don't want but are told they need to function—and in some cases survive.

There is a better answer. It is possible to live the life we desire and the one that God desires for us to have. We have to remember, no matter how cliché it sounds, **consistency is key.**

One Day at a Time

First, you have to take this one day at a time. Remember, when you mess up, it's okay. Get back on track as soon as you realize you've eaten one too many cookies or missed one too many workouts. Do not use that as an excuse to quit altogether. It's been said that those who are most successful are the ones who never quit. We will fail at times, but we will experience great results if we keep running the race.

> *"Do you not know that in a race all the runners run, but only one gets the prize? Run in such a way as to get the prize."*
>
> 1 CORINTHIANS 9:24, NIV

Give this new lifestyle your best effort, and keep your eye on the prize. You will never have victory over this battle if you continue to give up every time you experience frustrations. I don't know about you, but when I finish my race, I want the Lord to look me in the eye and say, "Well done thy good and faithful servant!" When we are faithful with little, we will be given much. That's not only in worldly possessions, but in greater responsibility and heavenly rewards as well. Do you want that for yourself? I know I do.

Change Comes Little By Little

Second, Stop looking at diets as a "fix it" for your life. Most of us have lived a fast-paced lifestyle, filling our bodies with fast food and grab-and-go meals from a box for many years. It takes time to change habits, and the gut microbiome. Once your gut has healed, you will get rid of food cravings, gas, bloating, and other physical ailments. Once you fix your gut, you'll experience changes in your outward appearance as your skin clears up, hair becomes silky, eyes brighten, and energy returns. This truly is a lifestyle change, and change is not always easy. It can be simple though. So, take a deep breath. Take one step at a time, and little by little you will become the healthier "you" that you're striving to be. Don't allow yourself to get overwhelmed. Right now, decide that you're going to make a list of things from this book you'd like to see yourself implement and grow into. Focus on the easiest things first and take it slow.

When things get tough (and they will), you need a solid "WHY" that drives you. Why did you start this new journey to better health? Do you want more energy to play with your kids, less irritability, an ideal body weight, or increased sex drive? There's a deeper reason you picked up this book. What is it? What is your why? Some have diseases or disorders they'd like to see improve or even reverse. Whatever your reason, it is possible. Write your "why" down along with your goals, and you'll be more likely to succeed and press forward.

I encourage you to pause right now and write down things you're missing out on today because of poor lifestyle choices that have led to sickness or disease. Use those as motivators for continuing on your path to wellness. It is worthwhile to create a vision board—cut out photos of you doing the things you want to do, the clothing you want to wear, the fitness level you want to have—and put those goals in front of your eyes every day. Meditate on them and you'll begin to see change. If you put them in front of you and see them on a regular basis, it will be easier to keep pushing toward that goal when the road gets tough. The Lord reminds me from His word to write the vision and make it plain (Habakkuk 2:2). When we put our vision down for us and others to see, it has a greater impact on our ability to change.

God's Desire for You to Live in Health

One of the most important lessons I've learned is that God does not want us to be sick, and He does not curse us with disease to teach us lessons. He is only good and loving and desires the best for us. Jesus died on that cross not only so we could have eternal life with our Heavenly Father, but also so we could live in health and prosperity. He didn't just die for our sins, but also for our sickness and disease. The belief that we have to eventually get sick before we die is a lie.

Does that mean we can live how we want and put anything in our body and expect to be well? No! We're responsible for the things we know, and when knowledge from the Word is revealed to us, we must act on it. I believe 100% in supernatural healing, but God will also show us how to prevent diabetes or heart disease from recurring if we follow His guidelines for treating our bodies as the temples they are. Joyce Meyer made a statement I will never forget: "We only have one body, and if we destroy it then we have to leave."

> *"Do you not know that your bodies are temples of the Holy Spirit, who is in you, whom you have received from God? You are not your own."*
>
> 1 CORINTHIANS 6:9, NIV

> *"Death and life are in the power of the tongue, and those who love it will eat its fruit."*
>
> PROVERBS 18:21, NKJV

This means we do not have to die from sickness or disease. As long as we take care of our vessels and refuse to accept sickness, we can live a full life until we're ready to go home ... and then we can just go. I fully intend to sit in my favorite place and ask God to take me when I know my time here is complete. I'll go in health, and what a glorious day it will be. I believe that's the way He intended it to be for all of His sons and daughters.

A Word of Caution

The information I share in this book is not to replace any medical advice you are currently receiving. I am in no way suggesting that you stop medications or adjust your own lifestyle patterns to follow what has specifically worked for me. The human body is much more complex than that. We all have different needs. This book is to simply have you think about some of the physical and spiritual toxins you are ingesting and see if small changes will help you. You are responsible for your own health. No one can do that for you— not even your medical practitioner.

"If you are not your own doctor, you are a fool."

HIPPOCRATES

I am simply passing along knowledge I once lacked to get well and stay well. So, grab a highlighter and mark the places in the book that make sense to you so you can seek advice from the Lord and your physician on how you could proceed if there are things you'd like to incorporate.

This book is not all-encompassing. I'll only touch the surface of the topics I found to be helpful on my healing journey. There are experts who can provide additional information that gets deep into the science of why these practices are important. You'll definitely hear more from me in the future as we dive deeper into some of the topics I present here. I have also shared some of my resources with you in the back of this book so you can research the information for yourself.

I highly recommend educating yourself in these areas as well as picking up your Bible and learning what God has to say. Make it a daily discipline. It's the greatest book in the world and God will use it to teach you everything you need to know. The secret is found in the words He speaks directly to you as you get to know Him. The only way to get to know Him is to spend time in His word and soaking in Him. This will help you learn to hear His voice. He has all the answers we need to survive and thrive. I pray as you seek Him that He'll reveal His wisdom to you where your own personal healing is concerned.

"If any of you lacks wisdom, you should ask God, who gives generously to all without finding fault, and it will be given to you."

JAMES 1:5 NIV

PREFACE

As I began to understand more about my healing journey to wholeness, I noticed that I would have dreams and visions of white horses. A day did not go by when I did not think of them, see them, or have someone bring up the subject of horses. I even met a horse rancher who offered me horseback riding at her ranch.

My visions usually involved me riding a white horse in the heavenlies, and oftentimes I was swinging a sword in the air like a warrior princess. I named myself as such (in the secret place of my own mind, of course) because that is what I felt like.

I know that God can speak to us through dreams, visions, and symbols too. There were just too many daily encounters with horses to ignore and I found it all a little peculiar, so I decided to research the meaning of horses. I learned that riding a horse indicates that a person will conquer their problems, rise to the top, and live a healthy life.

> *"So I looked and saw a white horse, and its rider had a bow. And he was given a crown, and rode out to conquer and defeat."*
>
> REVELATION 6:2, BSB

I also discovered that the white color of the horse was representative of the joy of knowing the power of God was on my side. This made perfect sense with the place I was in and brought great encouragement to me in my healing journey.

> *"Then I saw heaven standing open, and there before me was a white horse. And its rider is called Faithful and True. With righteousness He judges and wages war."*
>
> REVELATION 19:11, BSB

He is faithful and He is true. He opened the heavens before me, gave me a crown, and sent me out to conquer and defeat illness. I know now that I am a warrior who brings healing. I am faithful to what God is calling me to do, not only for myself, but for others as well. This vision was the next step that would take me right into my destiny.

CHAPTER ONE

How it All Began

I was brought up on the typical Standard American Diet. Blessed with grandparents and parents who had a garden, yard chickens, honey bees, and fruit trees, we were privileged to eat a lot of clean, fresh, whole foods. We also shopped at the local butcher and farmer's markets to fill in the gaps. But before you think we were health food nuts, I also remember loving those little packaged meals that included Hamburger Helper, frozen lasagna, and other sodium and preservative filled boxed varieties. For many years we had a weekly ritual of "Pizza Hut night" on Tuesdays between gymnastics and dance class. Friday nights were "family night," so we went to a restaurant and were sure to enjoy things like macaroni and cheese as well as ice cream with sprinkles for dessert. Like most families, we snacked regularly on chips and sodas and candy bars.

I remember having gastrointestinal issues as a child. My grandparents were aware of how important it was to poop regularly, so I received enemas on a consistent basis. When I started grade school, I was a little behind with reading abilities and had a hard time paying attention. No one attributed this to my diet. They just thought I was a slow learner. My dad, uncle, and a first cousin all had ADD/ADHD (Attention Deficit/Attention Deficit Hyperactivity Disorder) and I had been placed in that category as well. I made it through high school and went to college where my diet became much worse. I ate things like Minute Rice or peanut M&M's for dinner.

"Routine" Medications

I was prescribed birth control pills at the age of twelve to treat severe menstrual cramps. Because birth control disrupts regular hormone production in the body, I was also prescribed medication for depression—which I still question even today. As far as I was concerned, I never felt depressed, but this is a catch-all diagnosis many receive when there are hormone issues that doctors are unable to explain. So along with birth control pills and medication for ADD, they added a prescription for depression as well.

Early in college, I was diagnosed with irritable bowel syndrome (IBS), which required yet another medication. IBS is basically a nice way of saying, "We have no idea what's wrong with you." It's interesting now that I think back to this time because even though

I was having severe gastrointestinal (GI) symptoms that interfered with my daily life, I was never asked about my diet. One would think that diet may get brought up when there's a conversation regarding GI upset. The problem is, the majority of physicians don't consider dietary components when making a diagnosis since nutrition education constitutes less than one percent of their college curriculum.[1] It also includes the outdated food pyramid that we all have likely attempted to live by at one point in our lives. Anyone living on 11 servings of conventional grains a day is going to eventually experience some health problems.

ANYONE LIVING BY THE OUTDATED FOOD PYRAMID IS EVENTUALLY GOING TO EXPERIENCE HEALTH PROBLEMS

In college, I drank way too much alcohol—that's what college does to some—and at least a pot of coffee a day because I was exhausted all the time. I fell into the trap of self-medicating because I found it easier to focus on my studies that way. After graduation, I worked full time, and for much of the time held two jobs. I liked the extra money, but it eventually took a toll on my body. God kept telling me to slow down, but I wanted to keep going and be productive. I was an entrepreneur at heart, and learned that skill well from my dad. I continued this unhealthy pattern of activity without rest which led to a downward spiral in my health until I couldn't do it any longer. I had an "all or nothing" attitude. I had not yet learned the beauty of balance.

Desperate, I began researching my symptoms and after a little soul-searching, decided I wanted to get off all my medications. I had stressed my adrenals to the max from all the stimulants. I had also destroyed my thyroid function (which is common when we consume too much sugar and processed carbohydrates). I was losing hair by the hand-full. My progesterone and estradiol were out of balance because of the synthetic hormones I was prescribed as well as environmental toxins that interfere with hormone production. I was a complete hormonal mess.

Processed Food Junkie

I started eating organic, but I was a processed food and sugar junkie. This led to severe malnutrition. I later learned that this stemmed from a fungus or yeast overgrowth called Candida albicans. This was most likely due to overuse of antibiotics as a child along with birth control, and the consumption of too much processed junk food. I didn't know that this imbalance of bacteria in the gut was causing me to crave sugar and processed carbohydrates so they could thrive. These bugs are unbelievably smart, and these cravings were fueling their growth. Eventually, the bad bacteria outnumbered the good and infection spread throughout my entire body. Just like I didn't yet understand there was a healthy balance between work and rest, I also didn't know that for my gut health, the goal was that these bacteria should be in balance.

I wish I could fully explain all the symptoms I was facing at my weakest point, and I'll tell you more in the chapters to come, but I can tell you that the condition of my health was something I thought I would never get over. It seemed to get worse over time, no matter what I did. I lost tons of weight and felt like I could barely work a full day. I was underweight because I was malnourished (not everyone who is thin is healthy). In the afternoons, I would crash on the couch for a nap that was on average four hours.

Add to that skin issues like acne and eczema, which was super embarrassing, especially since I was in my mid-twenties. I had gallbladder attacks on a regular basis, which kept me from wanting to venture too far from home.

Looking for Answers

Looking back, I often wonder what if I had only eaten a real food diet with no prescription drugs? Would things have been different? I'm almost positive they would have. Like most people, neither my family nor I knew what these toxic or fake foods were doing to our bodies. We didn't understand the long term effects of drugs, antibiotics, GMOs (genetically modified organisms), and processed foods; nor did we know to ask. We still don't know all the side effects today, yet we continue to ingest them on a regular basis.

WE MUST EDUCATE OURSELVES ON THE TRUTHS INSTEAD OF RELYING ON BIG BUSINESS

What's the cost? Well, it's obvious that as a nation, we are becoming sicker and more overweight than ever. If we want that to change then we have to take matters into our own hands. We must educate ourselves on the truths instead of relying on big business to do it for us. Even if we live a healthy lifestyle, it is still important that we detox our bodies on a regular basis—this world is a very toxic place.

My journey began in desperation. I was sick and tired of being sick and tired. I wanted answers. I wanted energy. I wanted to feel good and be happy. Though I was trained as a nurse, I began to examine traditional medicine more closely. In the next chapter we'll talk about the role of physicians and pharmaceuticals and the importance of being educated and taking an active role in the direction of your own health.

"If someone wishes for good health, one must first ask oneself if he is ready to do away with the reasons for his illness. Only then is it possible to help him."

HIPPOCRATES

CHAPTER TWO

Today's Medicine
Where Have We Gone Wrong

"The doctor of the future will give no medicine, but will educate his patients in the care of the human frame, in diet, and in the cause and prevention of disease."

THOMAS EDISON

I went to nursing school because I had a desire to see others well. I knew doctors would prescribe an antibiotic when needed or perform a surgery for emergencies, but I had learned about natural therapies from my family and didn't expect that the medical field would be that much different. Boy, was I wrong! While in my clinical rotations, I realized that taking care of patients who were over-medicated and under-educated (about the reasons they were sick) was not a place I wanted to be forever. I did practice for a short period of time, but burn-out hit me quickly. I didn't understand why patients weren't informed about why they felt the way they did. Why were they on 2 or 3 different blood pressure medications and the same for diabetes? Why did all my patients have Metabolic Syndrome and no one was connecting that to poor lifestyle choices that they may not have even realized they were making? They needed dietary education and detoxification, not a handful of prescription drugs. What did I know though? I was not a complete picture of health myself, and I was just beginning to learn some of the things about which Western Medicine did not even touch the surface.

I didn't blame my patients, nor did I blame the doctors. I believe it was uneducated patients coming to undereducated (in some areas) physicians who knew a lot about treating the symptoms of disease but little about how to teach patients regarding a healthy lifestyle. They teach patients what they learn in medical school, and that's medicine—prescriptions and surgery. Most don't teach their patients to exercise or to meditate or to take a walk in the sunlight to relieve stress. Unfortunately, there's a pill for everything now. It saddens me to know that at the time of this writing, the third leading cause of death is medical error, yet we tend to trust modern medicine more than we do God's medicine. The Bible tells us that the Lord created medicines out of the earth and that their leaves are to be used for healing (Ezekiel 47:12).

I started to study a little about preventative care on my own because I realized there must be a better answer to experience wellness. The idea of preventing disease before it started seemed to make much more sense to me than trying to fix what was broken. A cardiac diet in Western Medicine means "no added salt." Now I

know salt is a wonderful addition to any diet, depending on the type you choose of course. Too much table salt will kill anyone. It's highly processed and stripped of nutrients. Pink Himalayan salt or Celtic sea salt is full of minerals and is a healthy addition to anyone's diet. Of course, these things are not common knowledge. The truth is, without the passion I gained for healing the human body naturally, I would have probably never learned these things either.

I spent countless hours studying and researching information on how to keep my body functioning at optimal levels. It's for that reason that I'm well today. I had been to countless doctors who provided no help in resolving my issues. I was exhausted to a point that I was willing to do anything to begin experiencing life again. There were simply no other answers in the medical arena except a new prescription for the latest miracle drug ... that I found no relief from taking. There are some great doctors out there, including the one I have helping me optimize my health, but it's been a long search to find someone who understands how to get to the root of the issue instead of just treating symptoms. I now realize that life without pharmaceuticals is possible with the right natural protocol.

Medical Practitioners and Pharmaceuticals

"Nearly all men die of their medicines, not of their diseases."

MOLIERE

There's a time and place for Western Medicine and the use of pharmaceuticals, but taking a pill for a medical condition has become the norm instead of the exception. We go to a physician who provides a diagnosis for which we expect some concoction to make it go away immediately. The questions should be, "Why am I experiencing this? Why have I developed these symptoms that have led to the diagnosis of a certain disease or disorder?" We don't even consider those questions though. We accept the diagnosis without question, trusting in the authority of the physician standing in front of us instead of trusting the Great Physician to provide us with the healing we so desire in our bodies. We have a pill for everything from a simple sniffle to more serious conditions like autoimmune disease and cancer. There are many problems associated with popping a pill for every little symptom we experience.

WE ACCEPT A DIAGNOSIS WITHOUT QUESTION

The body is very smart, and there are times we should let it do its job. Symptoms that come along with pain and inflammation are the body's natural response to something it sees as a potential invader. Inflammation is an overreaction of the immune system. It's an underlying cause of many disease processes. Medications and processed foods can add to the inflammation. The body has a very complex immune system that can fight off more than we give it credit for. We approach this with impatience though and ask for a pill before listening to what the body is trying to say. The pills may mask or even rid the body of those symptoms, but often come with a list of side effects in return. In the end, we've not treated the cause, we've only masked the symptoms of the disease process and allowed a chemical substance to produce even more issues for us to deal with in the long run.

In many cases, we take more drugs to treat those symptoms created by the initial drug. Before we know it we're making a trip to the pharmacy once a month to pick up a sack full of medications without really feeling well. Is that not the point of a medical treatment? Should we not expect it to make us feel completely well—not just give us a list of different symptoms to deal with and maybe a little relief? It is called "treatment" after all, right? We should expect more for the future of our health than this scenario described, but we all know someone who's experiencing this right now in their life. Sickness, disease, and the need for pharmaceuticals should not be the norm. We should not have to watch the majority of our loved ones become plagued by this vicious cycle.

The pharmaceutical industry is a huge money-maker. We see ads on television every day advertising new drugs. Even though they tell of the horrible side effects, we still go to our physicians and ask for them. Why? Because some of us are desperate for relief. Did you know there are physicians who are actually interested in helping you understand how to heal the body naturally? How to destroy your illness at the root? They look at your body and lifestyle, and examine you as an individual to make sure they understand what's causing your disease. They use prescription medications only when necessary. Their goal is to provide you with the tools to experience healing by use of a proper diet, exercise, and lifestyle changes. These physicians are called functional or alternative medicine doctors. They want to understand what's causing your symptoms and get to the root instead of masking the symptoms with the latest drug just to appease you.

We are partly to blame for this overmedicated life many of us live, due to the need for immediate gratification. We want that pill to just fix us. We expect medication when we go to a doctor's office. If we end up in an office where they don't give us what we want then we call them a quack. We then go to the next doctor to get our prescriptions, where someone is happy to write them.

On the other hand, there's a reason you are sick. It's not because you're Prozac deficient, and it's definitely not because your body is old. God never intended for us to become sick as we aged. We're not created to thrive for so many years and just fall apart before He decides to take us to relieve us from our misery. If you believe that, then you don't have a true understanding of the loving Father we serve. That's not part of the normal aging process or His plan for our lives. We should be able to live a long life in health.

We need to educate ourselves, and decide we're not going to add another drug to our list just because someone tells us we should. It's our job to ask physicians why they're prescribing a new medication. I encourage you to question your doctor if he or she is not interested in digging a little deeper to find out the reason for your sickness or symptoms. If we force them to treat us as individuals instead of "walking symptoms" then we could change the way medicine is practiced. They'll be forced to put their understanding of the human body to practice, or we'll take our business to those who are interested in helping us heal our whole body.

Second opinions and going with your gut instinct can be a real lifesaver when it comes to your health and the treatments you accept. I'm not telling you to dump your medications. Many times, it's dangerous to stop taking them without titrating down. Work with your physician, be it the one you have, or another medical professional who's willing to assist you in getting to the root of your disease. Once you learn what's causing the problem, it's easy to fix with a little work. I've watched countless individuals put an end to the need for medications, and the inconvenience and cost that comes along with them. Organic vegetables are much cheaper than expensive trips to the pharmacy and hospital bills. Choose Farmacy over Pharmacy!

I do have to end this section with a great story. It shows that even though many medical doctors do practice traditional medicine, they're willing to accept that pharmaceuticals are not always what's cutting edge. My grandfather spent fifteen years of his life on Coumadin therapy. He ended up having a stroke when he was almost 80 years old. He was in the hospital and my dad asked the doctor when he would be able to go home and how long it would take him to fully recover. His doctor told him that the likelihood of my grandfather getting much better was not good. My father found his answer unacceptable. He called in all the people he knew from the world of natural medicine, did his own quick research, and started his own protocol on my grandfather. This is not what I am recommending you do, but he literally dumped the medicines he was being brought by the nurse and fed him a handful of supplements in their place every day. He brought him nice foods and someone stayed with him at all times. Within a few days, he no longer had the excess blood on his brain and he was out of the hospital within two weeks.

The following week, a home nurse came to visit and he was outside cutting grass. She asked him what he was doing because he shouldn't have even been able to walk well at that point, much less do yard work. He told her the grass needed cutting so he was doing it. She ended up releasing him from her care after several visits of witnessing the same progress. A few months later, my grandfather received a knock on his door and it was his doctor—the one who said he would likely not function very well in daily life and would pretty much be a lifeless human-being. My dad showed up and the doctor wanted to know exactly what they had my grandfather on and how soon they started it after the stroke. He stayed for about an hour, wrote down all the information, and they haven't seen him since. He said he has never seen a patient recover like that and he had to know what caused the turnaround. We know God's hand was at work in this situation to bring my grandfather the healing he desired.

My family has always been intrigued by the human body, what it's capable of, and treating it with God's medicine for many generations now. That's exactly why this situation played out the way it did. My dad is not a doctor. He's simply a man who was not willing to accept the fact that lying in a bed with drool running down his face for the rest of his life was all my grandfather would be good for. He took matters into his own hands. Before long, my grandfather was back to the life of thriving that he once lived, and busier than many twenty-somethings I know. I can only hope that this doctor took some of that information and has been successful with other patients.

Cancer

"More people live off cancer than die from it."

DEEPAK CHOPRA

The acidic state of our bodies as well as hormone and nutritional deficiencies, stress, and toxins are major contributors to cancer. This is a condition we don't want to think of the possibility of receiving a diagnosis for in ourselves or loved ones. Some consider it a death sentence, but many have been enlightened to the fact that there's a different side of cancer treatment that doesn't involve the devastation we've all seen in the lives of our loved ones. There's another way outside the typical treatment of chemotherapy and radiation that makes patients so sick and kills what little immunity they have. There's more hope than we've been told when it comes to this dreaded diagnosis. It's really not a death sentence at all.

During my quest to better health, I was introduced to the work of Ty Bollinger, who now exposes the *Truth about Cancer* for the multi-billion dollar industry it is. I've heard many stories of people who have been given short periods of time to live and chose to seek alternative treatments over the death trap that chemotherapy and radiation offer. Guess what? They are still alive today to share their testimony. It's interesting to see the response of many oncologists when asked if they would provide the same treatments to their families or themselves if they received the dreaded cancer diagnosis. The majority of those asked said they would not subject their loved ones or self to those same treatments.

They would seek alternative therapies. Yet they pump patients full of this poison every day.

Truth be told, there is a cure for cancer, as well as most of the diseases people live with today. Unfortunately, there's no money in natural therapies like there is with chemo, because you cannot patent God's medicine. Chemo does improve symptoms because it destroys all the way down to the daughter cells, but cannot get down to the stem cells. That's the reason we can't get rid of cancer with chemo and we see it return in many patients. We're only masking it. I encourage you to look at Ty's work and many others who have exposed the pharmaceutical world for what it is. The cancer industry is just one of those areas.

> *"The thief's purpose is to steal and kill and destroy. My purpose is to give them a rich and satisfying life."*
>
> JOHN 10:10, NLT

Satan will use any means necessary to destroy us, even if it's tricking us into trusting that our care providers are presenting us with the best treatments available. I'm not saying you shouldn't trust your physician or saying they're only there for the money. There are many who care deeply about the lives of their patients. Just make sure you're aware of the alternatives before subjecting your body to the poisons that have become the standard of care. Our body is very smart and if we provide it with the natural things it needs in food, and supplements when necessary, then it will respond in a positive way and many times heal itself.

Vaccinations

"We have not lost faith, but have transferred it from God to the medical profession."

GEORGE BERNARD SHAW

The attempt to make vaccinations mandatory for all people is another area where pharmaceutical companies are teaming up with physicians and regulatory agencies to rake in your hard-earned money. I know this is a controversial topic, and no one can tell you whether or not to vaccinate. I will say that if you choose not to do so then it may not be an easy road for you. Make sure you understand why you've chosen that route and how you're going to handle it when faced with opposition. Not vaccinating is frowned upon by many, but I know for me, it's been a choice that has brought great outcomes—other than recently losing my job and half of our household income.

I had a religious and medical vaccination exemption on file for three years with a company. Going into my fourth year, they decided that was not going to work for them any longer. They gave me a brief time to make a decision as to whether or not I wanted to accept their toxins into my body and I politely declined their vaccinations. Within 21 days, I was without a job. So I will say again, if you make a decision that vaccinations are not for you then you may want to consider thinking about the worst thing that could happen to you for refusing. For me it was job loss, and that's probably the worst, right? It's not fun, but being a good steward of my body and my religious freedom means more to me than that. God has honored me for honoring Him.

Vaccinations are ever-increasing. Do a little research and you'll find that there are many more in the works that supposedly provide great protection from the diseases around us. How much do they really help, and how much do they really know? Two deaths out of a population of 8 million people is what started the smallpox craze.

HOW MUCH DO VACCINES REALLY HELP? WHAT DO THEY REALLY KNOW?

Why do we not question their uncertainty when we see the vaccination schedule change every few years as they pump these drugs into babies and young children? We look at the rise of ADD/ADHD and autism and other neurological disorders in children and really think it has nothing to do with this artificial manipulation of our body's own defense mechanism—the immune system. Physicians say we must do this if we want to be protected, and we're mistreated when we question them, as if we shouldn't have a choice. It saddens me greatly to see my family choose to vaccinate then end up calling to inform me they were sick for days after receiving a vaccination. Coincidence? You decide, but my earthly daddy says that our Heavenly Daddy speaks through coincidence.

There are great testimonies from "Moms against Vaccines," which is a group who shares stories of their own experience with the grueling vaccination schedule and the effect it has had on their children. "Vaxxed" is a movie that's dedicated to exposing the truth about vaccines. Many parents have watched their children become sick, seen neurological changes, and some even death within days or hours after receiving a vaccination. It's more prominent than some would imagine. If there are immediate effects like this then there are also long-term effects. There are even adults whose lives have been ruined over a simple flu vaccine that led to neurological changes in such a way that they've been deemed disabled. Those are a few examples, and yes there are many more—including my own.

I went to nursing school as a seemingly healthy individual, and that's pretty much where many of my severe problems began. As I was required to receive the flu shot, hepatitis B, MMR, Varicella, and TDap to start the nursing program, I accepted. I didn't attribute any of my symptoms to the vaccines at the time, but I definitely see the connection now. After the round of vaccinations, I started to notice a change in the way my brain was functioning. I couldn't think clearly, had difficulty finding my words, and felt like I was in a mental fog. I embarrassingly stuttered through my sentences at times because I literally couldn't verbalize what I was thinking. I had vision issues and felt as if my eyes were crossing.

I remember sitting in a lab one day and completely lost my vision in both eyes because of the strain I felt behind them. I had severe headaches that would often last for days at a time. My longest lasted for one month, but I had to pop my migraine medication and keep going. I had difficulty sleeping, irritability, and mood swings. These symptoms lasted for years. I'm so blessed that my husband even kept me around. I've come a long way since that time because I began detoxing my body, but it's been a long road. I'm now very passionate about the subject because I do see, looking back, that I was one of the "vaccine injured," likely from heavy metal toxicity. I'm grateful I've fully recovered from the symptoms.

So, yes! I will take job loss any day over going back to that place of cognitive decline. My employer didn't care though. They put me into the group of all the other individuals who were mandated to vaccinate. The problem is, we are individuals and what's good for one is not always good for another. In the case of vaccines, I see too much cover up and lies surrounding them and know the poisons that are in them and cannot believe it's legal to subject human beings to such things.

On top of the grueling schedule, these vaccines are filled with known toxins we are warned to avoid. They haven't been as preventative as they were thought to be with the recent outbreaks of the diseases these vaccines were supposed to protect from. Please don't blame the ones who choose not to vaccinate. That's a silly thought process when the vaccination should protect from any exposure—including vaccinated and unvaccinated individuals—if they worked as well as they claim. The CDC (Center for Disease Control) admits that flu shots fail half the time and that their efficacy rates decline with every vaccine a person receives.[1] If that's the case then I no more put anyone at risk than those who fall into the "failed vaccine" category. It's also been noted that those who are likely to report their general health status as "excellent" are unvaccinated individuals. Many of these diseases may have been eradicated by now if they weren't continuously introduced into the bodies of the majority of the population on a regular basis.

As I began to experience all the negative health effects from chemicals I'd been exposed to, my eyes were opened to the fact that vaccinations were not from God. He was not the creator of them and He has called me to live a natural life where I use no medications or medical treatments. He says I am more than a conqueror in Christ (Romans 8:28), so that means that I can overcome sickness with His help. He took on our infirmities, and carried our diseases (Matthew 8:17). The belief that we have to eventually get sick before we die is a lie. The belief that we need prevention in the form of a vaccine to avoid sickness is a lie. If we make the right choices and cleanse our bodies then we can live in health.

"But the fruit of the Holy Spirit is love, joy, peace, patience, kindness, gentleness, goodness, faithfulness, meekness, temperance; against such there is no law."

GALATIANS 5:22-23

This is who God is! These are the attributes we are entitled to. If I'm faced with a situation that requires a response from me, this is one of the first things I ask myself. Does the question at hand bring those Galatians 5 attributes to the surface? When it comes to vaccine policy, none of these come to the surface. I feel fear, pressure, evil, sickness, murder and greed. So my answer to the request becomes simple. God does not request anything that makes me feel any of the latter attributes, so I know for me, it's not from Him.

Most people have never asked what's in a vaccine. They trust the authority of the physician to give them things that will not harm them or their family. If you do choose to read a label insert, you'll find that they have some very interesting facts that should be explained to you by your physician before administering. They likely don't take the time though.

There was a time when I vaccinated and they never told me I was injecting aborted fetal cells, toxic levels of mercury in the form of thimerosal, foreign proteins from animals—which are responsible for several different types of cancer today, including brain and bone cancer, lymphomas, leukemia, and mesothelioma. What about the aluminum that's present in toxic levels? Or the formaldehyde, which is a known carcinogen? They surely never mentioned the benzethonium chloride, which causes seizures, coma, respiratory and central nervous system depression. Those are only a few, my friends.

Do you really think God designed all this and do you believe that He would force it upon His people knowing the potential harm it could cause? I know the answer to that and I'll tell you that my God would never subject His children to that. Scripture tells me that I am to keep my body free from toxic, foreign, and harmful substances. I am also not to submit to any governing authority which goes against the Word of God. I consider whole body healing a benefit and a blessing of the Lord and that's because I choose to live by and believe all that Matthew 6:33[2] has for me. It's time for Christians to realize that we don't have to accept the problems or ways of the world. We have a God who will teach us the way to go if we're willing to follow. The rules and laws will change if we all listen to Him, educate ourselves, and stand up for our beliefs and rights. They'll have no choice. We can put the Word of God on anything and see situations change. Even vaccination policy!

Reproduction—Women's Health

Our hormones need ample amounts of nutrients in order to work properly. They also need detoxification and more than a war zone inside our bodies to do their job. Most people consume hormone-filled meat on a regular basis, which also has a negative impact on their own hormones. Plastics and canned foods contain Bisphenol-A (BPA), Bisphenol-S (BPS) and other chemical-based plastic hardeners, which are major sources of our exposure to endocrine disruptors. Some other common exposures that impact hormones are lead from old paint, arsenic from tap water, mercury from fish, perfluorinated chemicals from non-stick pans, and fire retardants found in carpet and clothing. We come in contact with these toxins on a daily basis. Hormone imbalance can lead to symptoms like weight gain, mood swings, insomnia, depression, hair loss, lack of energy, water retention, brain fog, miscarriages, or inability to conceive. The list continues, depending on the hormones that are causing the issue.

I had a laundry list of these symptoms and more before finding a functional medicine doctor who could help get my hormones back on track. These symptoms can be avoided many times by consuming a balanced diet, avoiding as many hormone disruptors as possible, while detoxifying the body, and keeping up a daily exercise routine. It's important to cleanse the body of these hormone disruptors on a regular basis. Many times this detoxification process will naturally regulate hormones without the need to replace them.

I have a long history of hormone use. From the time I was in puberty, my gynecologist recommended I take birth control to help with unwanted symptoms of PMS (Premenstrual Syndrome). To all the women out there with PMS symptoms, there is hope for getting rid of this dreadful time you experience once a month for a week or longer. When your body is in a healthy state both physically and hormonally, your negative symptoms will disappear. No more cravings, bloating, water retention, severe cramping, mood swings, or anything else you experience every four weeks. Those around you will thank you too!

I was on birth control for about twenty years. I didn't realize my horrible symptoms were related to synthetic hormone use. When I put it all together, I stopped cold turkey. This may not have been the best idea, because it did wreak havoc on my body for several months, but I was ready to feel better at any cost. According to trusted functional medicine doctor, Dr. Robert Rakowski, the reason birth control works is because it messes up the hormones so bad that you couldn't get pregnant if you wanted to. Many doctors teach their patients that they mimic the human hormones, which isn't true.

The main problem with hormone replacement is that it causes your own body to stop producing its natural hormones. So in my case, my body was in that mess for about twenty years. My journey to hormonal health started with a little help of some natural plant-based hormones, best known as bioidentical hormone replacement therapy (BHRT). You may be in fear of hormone regulation because of the ties they've had with cancer and other diseases. This issue comes along with the use of synthetic hormones. We need to discuss the difference between synthetic and bioidentical hormones just in case you or your doctor feel there's no other way to regulate without replacement. Usually we can regulate our own if we clean up our system, but you may need them if you've had a hysterectomy or something of that nature.

Synthetic hormones are man-made from sources which are unnatural for human consumption. For instance, much of the synthetic estrogen is made from the urine of a pregnant mare. This makeup is not even similar to human estrogens and is about eight times times stronger. It tricks the body into thinking it's making estrogen. This causes the body to stop its own natural hormone production. If you think that's scary, then you should also know that birth control is 100 times as strong. These are hormones I would be afraid of and that's one of the reasons I stopped taking synthetic birth control. They are known to cause cancer and other disease states in the body.

SYNTHETIC HORMONES ARE KNOWN TO CAUSE CANCER AND OTHER DISEASE STATES IN THE BODY

Bioidenticals have the same molecular structure as the hormones produced in the body and cannot be differentiated by the body. They are plant-based and have been found to decrease the risk of certain cancers, especially breast cancer with estrogen and progesterone use. This is just an example of two of the body's hormones, but there are natural replacements for all hormones. BHRT is the safest way to obtain balance if you must have hormone replacement. If your doctor recommends replacement, but doesn't want to talk about these natural options, then I suggest getting a second opinion from one who understands the latest research on HRT. If at all possible, you should attempt to regulate them naturally. The reason is simple. You want your body to make its own instead of receiving a replacement, because that is what puts you in the most natural state. Give the body what it needs and it will give you what you need.

I spent many years on BHRT because that's what I knew as the best way to regulate hormones. I needed a quick way to help get me out of the slump I was in after twenty years of synthetic hormones entering my body. I was premenopausal at the age of twenty-seven. After about five years of BHRT, I noticed I needed more of the hormones to feel balanced and didn't see an end to the prescription drugs. I also didn't see my hormones reach optimal levels the entire time I was on therapy. I knew there was a better way, according to many of the professionals I respected in the field of functional medicine. That's when I learned just how much of an impact our environment has on our hormones.

We come into contact with hormone disruptors—in particular the Xenoestrogens which lead to estrogen toxicity. Xenoestrogens come from the environment in the form of toxins and imitate our natural estrogen. It causes a disruption in our natural hormone production. It's important to detox so we can rid the body of these disruptors. I met a functional medicine practitioner who did not believe HRT was necessary for me and showed me how to detox my excess Xenoestrogens to balance the body. The key is to find the right healthcare professional who will take as much care with your life as you do. He also assisted with nutrient regulation and has made sure I'm free from other toxins. I'm now on track to a healthier me without prescription drugs.

I'm not saying you'll never have to take another pill, powder, or supplement again, but the key is to put the right ones in the body so they get rid of the garbage, instead of taking those that are only helping with symptoms. Eating a nutrient-rich diet, controlling stress, getting plenty of sleep, along with resistance training are all great ways to improve hormone balance too.

Pregnancy and Birth

Many women have difficulty conceiving a baby because of hormone imbalance. This leads to expensive therapies as well as emotional and physical stress in attempt to one day have a baby. Hormone detoxification and balance is the answer for so many women who are in that place of despair. On the other hand, there are women who have no problems but choose to deliver via Cesarean section instead of vaginal delivery. Many women are opting out of vaginal deliveries and their physicians are allowing them to have elective C-sections, even when not medically necessary.

Passage through the birth canal is important for many reasons, but there are a couple that specifically relate to the health of the newborn and the child's future. The birth canal is a tight place for the baby, and helps squeeze out the amniotic fluid from the lungs. C-section babies do not get this extra squeeze, so they're typically suctioned by delivery staff to assist with the removal of as much mucus as possible.

In a vaginal delivery, the natural flora covers the baby in a film of good bacteria that's beneficial for healthy bacterial balance that will impact the baby for life. This doesn't happen in C-section deliveries and can lead to gut flora imbalances as the child ages. Many women who are unable to have vaginal deliveries due to medical reasons are soaking a sponge in the vaginal fluids and wiping the baby with it so they receive some of this beneficial bacteria. There are not enough studies to show how beneficial it is at this point, but there is active research being done. If you're reading this now and have delivered via C-section, then you can begin to replenish your child's healthy gut bacteria by giving them probiotics. It doesn't mean they are bound for an unhealthy life. I understand that many women don't have a choice, but these are a couple things to think about if you're one of those *opting* for C-section out of convenience.

Mammograms

Mammograms are another controversial topic, since most medical doctors push women into sitting through this painful process. This is something I've never wanted to do, but now that I know the truth about them, I'm glad I haven't reached that point. My research prevented me from ever getting one. When we smash the breasts in between the plates used for mammogram, it can cause physical trauma and inflammation. Mammograms also use radiation, and women who receive regular mammograms have a higher rate of cancer.[3]

Cancer appears as a clump of abnormal cells. When those cancerous cells are broken up through biopsy, it increases the risk for metastasis because the cancer cells that break free can travel to other areas in the body and begin to grow. That could explain the high rate of metastasis associated with breast cancer.

Thermography is a safe alternative. It's a thermal imaging diagnostic technique that's also more accurate and less painful than mammograms. So, when you are ready for your next mammogram, ask your doctor if this is an available option or find someone who uses this technology.

Mental and Emotional Health

Every treatment in this book can, in some way, help with mood disorders. Depression usually begins when people start focusing on themselves and their current situation. It's a real condition, but truly is an attack from the enemy and can be removed from our lives when we seek God and keep our eyes on Him instead of our situation. Again, we want to get to the root of the depression when praying for someone who is battling this stronghold.

"And now, dear brothers and sisters, one final thing. **Fix your thoughts on what is true, and honorable, and right, and pure, and lovely, and admirable. Think about things that are excellent and worthy of praise."**

PHILIPPIANS 4:8, NLT (EMPHASIS ADDED)

Depression is a common diagnosis when men or women (especially women) approach their physicians about the hormone-related symptoms they have in the beginning stages of hormone decline. It's a common go-to diagnosis when medical professionals are unable to explain physiological symptoms. They blame the high stress lives we live, give us antidepressants, and tell us we need to take some time to relax. I've seen it over and over. They make us think we are crazy!

Many of us do live in a high stress state. From our jobs, to finances, dysfunctional families, lack of sleep, and little time to take care of our bodies, we end up in an emotional mess. Most everything mentioned in this book has a great impact on our emotional health. That doesn't mean we're depressed though. Nor does it mean we should take a medication for it. When a person is stressed, it should be dealt with at the root. Too often it's treated at a surface level, looking only at the symptom, which we physically see as the lack of drive or enthusiasm for life.

There are other types of mental health issues that can be caused from poor dietary choices. I personally suffered from insecurity and irritability when I was consuming gluten. It sounds silly, but my confidence levels are not as high when my brain is functioning slower than I know it should. I've eliminated grains from my diet, but if I sneak some in, I can tell immediately. Within half an hour, I feel irritable, groggy, and lose my zeal for life. It's a terrible feeling that always leads me to say, "I am never eating that again!" Some people do experience depression from these same foods.

Many times, people receive a pill for depression, one for anxiety, and one to help them sleep. Then they self-medicate with a glass of wine at night to wind down. There are proven natural remedies for symptoms of depression, anxiety, and even schizophrenia. Did you know that exercise has proven to be more effective than Prozac for depression?[4] You may also be shocked to know that there are cases of schizophrenia, autism, and depression that have gone away with a change in a person's diet.[5]

Another big player in depression is in a person's vitamin D levels.[6] It's been shown that many of those suffering from chronic disease or mental illness have insufficient vitamin D levels. It's amazing what the body is capable of when we give it what it needs. I'm not saying that depression and anxiety are not real, because I know firsthand they are. I also know that getting to the root, which many times is a toxic system, will clean up these disorders in many people. Check out the work of Certified Nutritionist, Trudy Scott, for help in finding the root to your mood disorders.

> IT'S AMAZING WHAT THE BODY IS CAPABLE OF WHEN WE GIVE IT WHAT IT NEEDS

On another note, many people use food for pleasure to the extent that they overeat to fill a void. Emotional eating sometimes comes from a place of escape or pain. It can also be a way for others to hide behind their food so they're not noticed. There are many women of sexual or physical abuse who actually feel safe when they're overweight. There's an underlying belief that they're protected from others if they appear undesirable. The psychology of eating is not considered by some to be important, but many of us shame ourselves when we have a piece of cake. We make excuses as to how we are incapable of passing it up.

If we want a piece of cake now and then, we should have it and absolutely enjoy it to its fullest. There are even great recipes online for healthier options that are delicious. There's a line we must draw with the amount of cake we eat to remain healthy, but it's okay to enjoy a sweet treat now and then. I do recommend finding recipes for healthier dessert options and sticking with those so you avoid all the harmful additives that are in the store bought varieties, but don't punish yourself for eating a piece of Aunt Sally's birthday cake if you want it. I do suggest you take notice in how you feel afterwards though. You may find it's not really worth it. If it is though, then make sure you guiltlessly enjoy it.

In the next chapter we are going to take a more in-depth look at food and nutrition and the role it plays in our health.

"Let thy food be thy medicine and medicine be thy food."

HIPPOCRATES

CHAPTER THREE

Food and Nutrition

"Eat real food. Not too much. Mostly Plants."

MICHAEL POLLAN

The purpose of food is to provide the body with adequate nutrition to allow us to function full of energy on a daily basis. Many people look to the quickest and most convenient food-like substance available to tide them over until they must eat again. Others look for what they believe to be the most delicious, not considering the nutritional value of the food. We often don't think about what we're putting into our bodies or how it's going to make us feel. We don't recognize the difference between real food and faux food. We choose a bag of chips over an apple with almond butter for a quick snack, when the latter could provide us with so many more nutrients, natural hydration, that satisfying crunch, and fresh taste. Our taste buds have been developed to prefer artificial flavors over real food. This is just one example, but we must begin to pay attention to what we feed our cells if we want to look and feel our best and live without disease. The Bible give us a great idea about what God intended for us to eat:

> *Then God said, "I give you every seed-bearing plant on the face of the whole earth and every tree that has fruit with seed in it. They will be yours for food."*
>
> GENESIS 1:29, NIV

> *"Of all the animals that live on land, these are the ones you may eat: You may eat any animal that has a divided hoof and that chews the cud."*
>
> LEVITICUS 11:2-3,NIV

In these passages He tells us about the meat and plants that are available to us for food. God gave us plenty of whole, living foods to sustain us. Our food industry has chosen to destroy even some of those whole food options though.

We must begin to consider more than how great something tastes and start looking at food as nourishment to the body. Of course, fast food and sugar-filled treats may make up a great percentage of the foods you consume today, so these are the types of foods you have a taste for. Companies pay people great money to make sure their consumers find the foods they produce addicting so they're sure to have repeat customers.

Fast food is convenient, but not healthy, no matter how much their marketing campaigns try to tell us otherwise. The fish sandwich on the menu at McDonald's is no better than the hamburger. They are both filled with preservatives and unnecessary ingredients that deteriorate our bodies and destroy our health in the long-run. The best option is skipping the drive-through altogether. Once you begin to fill your plate with more nutritious alternatives, you'll find your taste buds quickly change and soon you'll be disgusted by those fast food choices.

Taste has to be cultivated. Don't worry if you don't love a healthy choice the first time you try it. There are some foods I've not been too fond of in the past, but I know God intended for me to receive nutritional value from a variety foods so I purposely incorporated them until I acquired a taste for them. If you'll make a practice to remove one bad food and replace it with a healthier option, you'll find your taste buds start to change over time. I remember a time when I found enjoyment in eating Popeye's chicken or Wendy's burger and fries. I could not imagine eating either of those now. I have a friend who lives and breathes nutrition who says he would not even drink the *water* from McDonald's. For the most part, I agree with him.

Many times those grab and go meals from a fast food or convenience store also cause gastrointestinal distress because of the combination of foods we're eating in one sitting. Some people may not have a problem when it comes to digesting certain foods together, but food combining has given many people relief from GI distress when choosing to properly combine their foods. For example, meat and fat are not easily digested with starchy carbohydrates. They compete for the necessary digestive enzymes that break down our food so it can be appropriately used by the body. That can explain the very heavy, full feeling we get when eating a steak and potato together or spaghetti with meat sauce. Since these food groups are not easily digested when eaten together, protein and fat should be eaten separately from starchy carbohydrates. In other words, eat carbs with carbs. This means you can have potatoes or pasta (if you choose to eat it) with any other vegetable you like. Meat protein can be eaten with any other food type, like fats or non-starchy vegetables. These decisions will lead to better digestion and a happier gut.

On my journey to health, I tried almost every fad diet out there. With every new fad, I thought, "well this is what I've been missing, and this is why I couldn't get well before." Some of these diets work for a period of time, but eventually we go back to our old habits. There are many people preaching "lifestyle change," and that's exactly what's needed. We have to take responsibility for our own mindsets. This is one of the most important truths in your healing process. Pay now, by sacrificing your fleshly desires, or pay later in poor health and medical bills. The choice is yours. The best diet for one person may not be what's best for another. Every person should eat carbs, fats, and proteins, as well as consume micronutrients in the proportions that make them feel best. Some people may not need much meat protein, while others don't feel well without it. Find what works for you and stick with that.

Some are also obsessed with labels, like "I am a vegan," or "I am Paleo." Someone can eat a very unhealthy diet of chips and sodas and call themselves a vegan without even taking in vegetables. Think about the limitations of these labels. When we label ourselves, it puts us in a box. It prevents us from venturing out and making choices that are most beneficial for our health. Not to mention that if we fail to hold true to that label, we feel guilty. Associating guilt with food has a negative impact that can lead to unhealthy eating patterns that are emotion-based. Be careful with these labels. It could be part of the reason you are at a standstill.

ASSOCIATING GUILT WITH FOOD HAS A NEGATIVE IMPACT THAT CAN LEAD TO UNHEALTHY EATING PATTERNS

I highly respect people who can admit openly when they make a mistake, especially when it comes to such a drastic lifestyle change. Check out Kristen Suzanne's blog. She's an ex-vegan, who lived that lifestyle most of her life. She wrote books helping others live the lifestyle as well. Her once ignored decline in health as well as the health needs of her family led her to start including clean meat in her diet. It was a very difficult change for her family, but the results were outstanding. Our bodies all have different needs, and there's no one size fits all diet. We have to listen to our bodies and make decisions for ourselves based on how we feel. Your body will let you know if a food type is right for you. Food should make us thrive, and if you're tired after consuming any particular food or food group then you should strongly consider the fact that it may not be serving your body.

Think about where your nutrients are coming from. That doesn't mean you can take a handful of supplements and continue eating a poor diet. You need a wide range of foods to make sure you're satiated and able to resist cravings later in the day. You'll likely rid the body of cravings completely if you're giving it what it needs to thrive. We're so used to eating out and allowing someone else to take responsibility for preparing our meals. We don't even know what we're eating. We consume it and hope it gives us what we need.

Most restaurants use the cheapest ingredients possible that will provide an acceptable flavor to your palette, which has been adjusted because we eat so many preservative-filled foods. They take real food and smother it in sauces, fry it in cheap oils, and serve it with a side of processed starch. The portions are about double the amount of food that any one person should take in at one meal. It's a disaster in a bag or on a plate, and we actually pay people to serve it to us.

Remember, we create our food industry by what we purchase and consume. When there is more of a demand for organic vegetables and clean meats then we'll see those foods become more accessible and better priced. Most of the time you'll be able to find a local restaurant that uses local food when possible and even serves organic produce and clean meats. They cook nourishing foods and offer great options when you want a meal away from home. You can play it safe by ordering steamed vegetables with a sweet potato, and avoid foods that are battered or cooked in oils.

Processed Foods

The type of food we consume is a key factor in becoming healthy. You can exercise all day but you can't out-exercise a bad diet. I have to agree with some of the well-respected nutritionists when they say, "abs are made in the kitchen." We have to realize that food companies are not on our side. They've created processed foods with robust, artificial flavors so we no longer find whole foods appealing due to what we now consider a bland taste after constant consumption of food alternatives. Processed foods are filled with chemicals and unnecessary fillers that most of us cannot pronounce. The only thing they're good for is sucking our energy, depleting us of nutrients, and creating food addictions. The added chemicals in our foods do give it flavor, but why are we willing to sacrifice our health for it when we have so many natural spices that give us the ability to liven up the flavor of our dishes in a much cleaner way? Why are we eating dead food and expecting it to give us life?

If you'll take the next step to remove processed foods from your diet, you'll realize how much better tasting whole foods are over their lifeless alternatives. It will take time, but if you stick with it, you'll begin to wonder how you ever passed up a beautiful vegetable dish for a fast food burger. I know your main excuses are likely lack of time and energy, and they'll continue to be until you determine to make a change. Every one of us have the same amount of time in a day, and millions choose to create a healthy lifestyle while others resist it. You have to make the decision to set aside time to prepare how you will receive proper nutrients to fuel your busy life. You'll find that making healthy meals is quick and easy with a little practice. It's the only way out of the vicious cycle—where lack of energy continues with processed food consumption. Bad habits are hard to break, but no one can do it for you. I know, because I was a woman of many bad habits that I had no intention of breaking until it became necessary.

There's a simple phrase I picked up from another author and educator who talks about healing our bodies with natural foods. Jack Lalanne said, "If God didn't make it then don't eat it." This is very simple to say, but do we really understand what that means? If it comes from a box from the center aisle at the grocery store, you probably shouldn't be eating it—or at least not as a dietary staple. Of course the packaging says all natural! What does that mean anyway? Why are we trusting the ones collecting our money to tell us if what they're selling is really healthy? If you think they care more about your health than they do that bottom dollar then you're sadly mistaken. If you think the food labeling laws are made to protect you as the consumer then that's another mistake.

> "IF GOD DIDN'T MAKE IT THEN DON'T EAT IT."
>
> —JACK LALANNE

I would suggest looking at the ingredients on all the processed foods you buy, including canned sauces and vegetables. If you see ingredients you can't pronounce, don't buy it. Maybe there will be words on the label that you can pronounce, but many of those are still unnecessary ingredients and toxic. So I warn you to be careful about purchasing products that say red or yellow #, caramel coloring, high fructose corn syrup, hydrogenated oils, or other items that you do not recognize to be real food. I encourage you to do some research on what's safe and purchase only those things. Don't just look at the front of the box for your ingredient information. I have a friend who picked up a box of crackers one day and ate them for days. She came into work one day and complained of her fatigue and swelling and said she felt as if she'd been exposed to gluten. She finally read the box and found wheat to be the main ingredient in a box of crackers that had a gluten-free label on the front. Be careful with these confusing labels that are made to trick consumers.

The fillers in processed foods are the cause of many cognitive problems and are carcinogenic—meaning they cause cancer. Natural flavors can also be anything that occurs in nature. Do you know that some natural flavors include beaver anal secretions? I do not know about you, but that's not something I care to purposely ingest. I encourage you to check out the US Food and Drug Administration to see exactly what their definition is regarding natural flavors.[1] It's shocking to say the least. Many processed foods don't have an all-inclusive list of ingredients on the label. This is the case for foods that are Generally Recognized As Safe (GRAS), so they don't require a food label. Just because they're GRAS doesn't mean I want them in my body. It's obvious we cannot trust the people making those decisions.

It's interesting to look at food ingredients. Especially in some of the major chain restaurants and companies like Kraft. Many of the poor toxic ingredients that are in the products in the USA versus other countries may shock you. For example, in the UK, McDonald's French fries have potatoes, vegetable oil, dextrose sugar, and salt. In the USA, those same french fries have all the ingredients listed as well as hydrogenated vegetable oil, artificial beef flavoring from hydrolyzed wheat and hydrolyzed milk, citric acid pyrophosphate, dimethylpolysiloxane, and tertbutylhydroquinone. I'm not saying either option is a healthy one, but why all the unnecessary extras in the French fries made for the USA? One reason is because we allow it, while many other countries forbid the use of these ingredients. There are food advocates like Vani Hari, also known as the Food Babe, who have made great strides to speak out for the people and protect what's on our plates. Either way, I don't believe fast food is an acceptable option, but for those of you who won't have it any other way, you can thank those like Vani for their dedicated work to bring forth the truth in an attempt to hold these companies responsible for what they're serving.

We've heard to shop on the perimeter of the store to choose the healthiest foods. This is for the most part true, as it is where fruits, vegetables, and meats live. You'll also find the cooler section with cold juices, which are most of the time unhealthy options. Many of them say "fresh-pressed" and have seemingly healthy ingredients, but be careful with sugar content in those "healthy green drinks" you purchase at the supermarket. When you check out the ingredients, look for things like apple juice compared to apple juice concentrate. A lot of times, the extra sugar comes from the simple fact that they've added a juice concentrate instead of a whole food. When purchasing juices that are already bottled, choose organic, cold-pressed, high pressure processed, and make sure there are no non-food ingredients. There are still important things to remember when choosing whole foods, so we'll now look a little closer at some of the food options we have and how to choose the best ones.

Fermented Foods

Eating fermented food is especially good for the gut and can reverse disease. Our gut is full of an array of bacteria. With our typical Standard American Diet, overuse of antibiotics, and constant contact with the toxins around us, the balance in our gut bacteria can become disrupted. We can change the gut environment by purposely adding these healthy bacteria back in through fermented foods. They also help boost the immune system and are potent detoxifiers. Cleaning up the gut bacteria can have a positive impact on obesity, autism, diabetes, mood, and behavior.

FERMENTED FOODS TOP MY LIST FOR THOSE WITH POTENTIAL TO CHANGE A PERSON'S LIFE

If I had to choose one food that really has the potential to change a person's life, then I would have to say that fermented foods is at the top of that list. That and bone broth run a really close race. Our ancestors included fermented foods in their diets on a regular basis. This is partially because they needed a way to preserve foods and didn't have refrigeration to keep things fresh like we do today. Now we can buy live cultures to create our own fermented foods, or we can buy things like sauerkraut or kimchi at a local grocer.

Make sure you're buying these from the cooler section of your grocery store and not from the shelves. Also make sure your sauerkraut contains live cultures. The kraut found on the shelves at grocery stores, which many people put on hot dogs, doesn't contain live cultures. Other cultured foods include things like yogurt, kombucha, and kefir. I like to rotate between several brands, and even make my own sauerkraut and kombucha in large batches to get a range of bacteria. There are culture starter kits you can purchase if you decide to make your own, as well as recipes online.

Kombucha is a fermented tea that has gained popularity recently. I never realized how much fun it would be to grow my own little SCOBY (Symbiotic Culture of Bacteria and Yeast) for kombucha tea and keep it alive and grow babies and share health with others by sharing my brews. It's been such a delight in my life. It's like having a garden. Watching it grow from a few simple ingredients to a healthy beverage is amazing. If you think the kombucha from the store is good, then you'll love the homemade version. I remember the first time my husband tasted our homemade kombucha. He said, "Wow! That is delicious!" If you knew my husband then you would know he doesn't tend to get overly excited about much. He definitely doesn't get that excited over the store-bought version. My dad also makes homemade kombucha and said he downed half a gallon immediately after he finished brewing his first batch. It is amazing stuff for sure. Plus it has billions of healthy little creatures for your gut health living right in it.

I did mention yogurt as a food with live cultures. You can usually find yogurt made from coconut, dairy cows, or goats. You can even find grass-fed options. You've likely heard that eating yogurt is good for you. While I don't disagree entirely, I do see the benefits if it's from healthy sources and is not full of added ingredients. We will discuss this a little more later, but I'm a firm believer that dairy can be more harmful than beneficial if it's from conventionally raised animals. Most yogurt is full of added preservatives and sugar alternatives, which also do more harm than good. With the increase in popularity of yogurt, this food sometimes has an aisle of its own at the grocery store with more choices than we care to imagine. I definitely would not consider the majority of those to be health foods.

Should I Eat Organic?

There are many reasons people quickly dismiss the importance of eating organic. It concerns many of us that even our organic crops are being contaminated by the conventional pesticide-laden crops. This is a real issue. There's no way we can get away from pesticides completely, but when eating organic we can rest assured that the food was not purposely sprayed with unnecessary chemicals. The amount of toxins is much less in organic foods. According to the research, there is a real difference in toxic burden on the body when consuming organic over inorganic foods.[2] There are also plant-based foods that are more likely to have higher pesticide levels than conventional ones. Check out the dirty dozen online to determine which fruits and vegetables you should buy organic, and the clean 15 for the ones that are less likely to hold on to those pesticides. This will help you save a little money when grocery shopping if you feel you cannot afford to buy all organic items. Once your body rids itself of some of the toxins associated with poor quality foods, your grocery bill goes down. This is not only because you'll be satisfied on less food, but also because processed food is more expensive.

Purchasing organic food does seem expensive when looking at it from a glance. Many of the pesticide-laden produce, grain-fed meat, and processed foods don't satisfy the body for extended periods of time like whole foods can. I know it sounds silly, but if we provide the body with the proper balance of nutrients, then we can live on less food. Our bodies are really looking for nutrition, not just calories. Many processed foods, even in their organic form, have a negative impact on blood sugar levels. This is especially true with grains. When blood sugar levels drop, it signals ghrelin, which is the hunger hormone that tells us it's time to eat. When we eat clean foods, we receive the nutrients we need along with extra fiber, which is very satiating for longer periods of time.

The chemicals in conventional foods often lead to sickness and disease and can negatively impact every organ system in the body. They can lead to things like cellulite (from toxins in our fat storage), brain fog, eczema, poor circulation, brittle hair and nails, low energy, hormone imbalance, and mood swings. They can also lead to neurological impairment, depression, and anxiety. There are a multitude of ways toxins impact the body, and I'm willing to bet we've not even touched the surface with the little bit of knowledge we have surrounding the subject. We're already exposed to way too many toxins on a daily basis that we have no control over. It's detrimental to your health to choose to ingest additional toxins on a daily basis, especially when very few people follow a regular detox protocol.

If you listen to companies like Monsanto and some of their spokespersons, you'll hear that pesticides and GMOs are safe and that there's no harm in eating them. The problem with the study of pesticides is that they're studied in isolated environments and for short periods of time. They never study the effects of multiple types of pesticides together. Where they may only have small negative impacts alone, they have compounding negative effects when in combination. In other words, these studies are flawed. I'm passionate about helping others understand the importance of eating organic foods because I've watched the positive impact it's had on those I love most, including myself.

My husband started a travel role about five years after we started eating an all organic diet, filled with colorful vegetables and clean protein. Although he never gave up grains and dairy entirely, he was in a much healthier state than before. His body was very happy with the changes. He stopped experiencing sinus infections, gained more energy, and lived a life of vibrancy. He was ingesting food that was full of of life, and his body was telling him in many ways that it was happy with his choices.

His new role required that he travel most of the time and we only saw each other every couple of weeks. I noticed major changes in his health and watched for a while, waiting for him to notice as well. I knew by looking at him that his diet was not what it should be. He started to gain excess body fat around the abdomen. He began having allergic reactions with the change of the seasons again, which had no longer affected him with a cleaner diet. He had bags under his eyes, and inflammation that was noticeable in his swollen face and extremities. These were only a few of the signs of toxicity that were showing me his health was declining.

This went on for about nine months. Then we sat down as a couple and realized we both were concerned with his state of health. Since then, he has made changes that have impacted him in a positive way. He's removed many of the processed foods from his diet, and has even purchased a grill to keep on the back of his truck so he can cook healthier foods in the evenings. He does still eat out, but is cognizant of the choices he makes. He's even finding enjoyment in getting back to his healthier lifestyle. He didn't realize what he was missing until he began to taste health again.

These changes didn't come easy for him though. It wasn't fun at first to hear he was going to have to put a little effort forth to live in health. It's definitely easier to sit in a restaurant and have someone serve you and to choose those comfort foods when away from home and loved ones. It's even easy to find emotional support in those foods. As healthy of a lifestyle as I live, I realized during this time that I could not live it for anyone but myself. It's hard to watch someone you love so much go through this, but we as individuals are responsible for our own health. You can only do it for yourself.

My body and taste buds know when I've eaten heavy pesticide-laden foods. Take a simple raw salad, for example. Whether it be from a salad bar in a cafeteria or a chain restaurant, I can taste the poisons (that's what I call them) from the moment they touch my tongue. If I do decide to finish the salad, I regret it later because it zaps my energy, causes gas and bloating, drowsiness, brain fog, and other unwanted effects in my body. Most people probably don't find an issue with the taste, but it's something I'm very sensitive to because ninety-five percent of my diet is organic. I try not to be too picky when eating out with a group, but it seems like many times when I go into a restaurant and even order the cleanest looking item on the menu, it turns me into a zombie within a few hours. I would much rather prepare my own meals and know what's on my plate.

It frustrates me that restaurants even serve the junk and charge for it. Again, it's all about that bottom dollar and we as consumers are accepting it with no complaints. We should expect more, and these restaurants should take a little more pride in the quality of the food they serve. I stopped eating fast food many years ago, and have removed most chain restaurants as well. Eating from my own kitchen is not always possible, because I spend much of my time in airports, hotels, and hospitals with my current job. I cook a lot of my own food and pack it, but there are times when I end up in a restaurant. When that happens, my advice is to avoid what is tempting and go with something simple.

There are USDA Certified Organic foods available at most grocery stores now. These foods are guaranteed to be 95-100% organic and not genetically modified. They cannot guarantee 100% organic because of the use of pesticides on nearby farms, which can travel to organic farms by way of wind or natural water sources. There are also places to shop online that will deliver produce and meat directly to your doorstep. A great way to save money would be to grow your own organic foods and start a small garden for personal consumption. There are many ideas online to help you get started, and require very little maintenance.

If you decide to start your own garden, make sure you purchase organic seeds or starter plants so your foods are as clean as possible. Many times you'll find produce that doesn't have the USDA certified organic sticker on it, but it has a label that says it's organic. Smaller companies don't always go through the process to get certified by the USDA because it's expensive and has very strict rules. You'll have to make a decision regarding whether or not you only want to purchase USDA certified foods or if you trust the local farmers. I typically purchase those that are not certified when that's what's available, but you can refer back to the dirty dozen to help you with which ones you should purchase only in their organic form. Many times you can taste the difference too.

Shopping at local farmer's markets or grocery stores is a great option to make sure you're buying seasonal vegetables and getting the best price. At farmer's markets, you're usually able to speak directly with the farmer and can ask questions about how they grow their produce. The food we purchase in grocery stores is likely picked before it's ripe so it has time to travel to stores without going bad before it ends up on our plate. The problem with the produce not being ripened on the vine is that the nutrient content suffers when it's picked early.

Buying local ensures that you're getting the freshest produce possible. Many times you'll be able to find vine-ripened produce, which is the most flavorful in my opinion. Plus it supports your local farmers. You may find that your local farms have organic produce as well. I've moved around a good bit, but have always managed to find local farms, even many that will deliver right to your doorstep. If these places are difficult to find near you, then you can order boxes of produce and meat online and have it delivered to your door. You can also find places that will deliver healthy prepared meals if convenience is what you're looking for. I have a few places listed in the back of the book for your convenience.

Understanding GMOs

GMOs are genetically modified organisms. It means the food has been genetically manipulated in a lab, usually for the purpose of being able to withstand the herbicides and pesticides the plant is sprayed with. Genesis 1:11-12 tells us that we should yield fruit of their *own* kind. This manipulation is not what God intended. The excuse companies use for creating GMOs is that it takes this process to be able to feed the planet and prevent world hunger. How could this excuse be anything other than a cover-up, considering the amount of food that's thrown away daily? Organic testing has shown that we could more than double the amount of food produced if it was all grown organically. Even though most don't consider GMOs safe for consumption, there's no mandate placed on food companies to label them.

Genetically modified ingredients are found in more than 70 percent of processed foods. The Non-GMO Project chooses to keep consumers informed and verifies foods as non-GMO in hopes that companies will stop producing consumables that contain GMOs. You can look for their label on foods they've tested that have proved to be non-GMO. Most produce is pretty safe, but some of the top genetically modified ingredients to look for are soy, cottonseed, corn, canola, Hawaiian papaya, tomatoes, alfalfa, sugar beets, conventional dairy, squash, zucchini, and aspartame.

Organic and Non-GMO: What's the Difference?

Non-GMO is exactly what it says—it does not contain GMOs. Organic foods are also non-GMO, but they don't contain herbicides, pesticides, human waste, endocrine disruptors, heavy metals, or antibiotics. Just because it says organic doesn't mean it's healthy though. Think about all the organic snack or meal replacement bars that are still loaded with tons of "organic cane sugar." You still need to read the labels to make sure you're aware of what's in your food. Even eating too much "organic" sugar is not good for anyone's health.

The FDA has now approved GMO salmon. This could lead to contamination of other salmon in open waters. Without proper testing, we could unknowingly be consuming GMO fish. GMOs are not safe. *Genetic Roulette* by Jeffrey Smith is a great movie for those interested in learning of the adverse effects in the body when GMOs are consumed. They've been found to cause tumors, liver and kidney damage, organ failure, allergic reactions, and even premature death. It's important that we get involved and take a stand for what's happening to our foods. There's much room for improvement where the contamination of our food is concerned. We all play a major role in fighting back. One easy way to do so is to contact your senators so your voice can be heard. You can also keep up with the latest petitions for your rights at www.change.org.

You have a right to clean food and to know what you're putting in your body. The allowance of mislabeled or unlabeled genetically engineered foods is sickening when they have such a negative impact on the health of the entire world population. We're also responsible for praying for areas where change is needed. God hears our cries and He wants to give us the desires of our heart. We can literally move mountains with prayer. He's fully capable of turning this food contamination issue around. There are plenty of truths in His word that remind us that He is a good and giving God. If He is going to feed the birds healthy eats and not let them go hungry then how much greater will He provide for His children (Matthew 7:11)? The birds do not compare to how important we are.

Speaking of animals, there have been studies where different animal species were given the option between GMO or non-GMO feed and have left the GMO feed untouched.[3] If these animals are smart enough to leave it alone, then we should definitely do the same.

Another toxin in our food worth mentioning is Bacillus thuringiensis (BT). It's a bacteria that produces a protein that's toxic to insects. BT is a widely used pesticide that causes the stomach of a bug to explode when they ingest this poison. Monsanto claims it's safe for human consumption when it's sprayed on our plants, as it's only harmful to the bugs. The studies have revealed something quite different than their claims though. BT toxin has a similar effect on humans as it does bugs when consumed. It's one of the causes of something called Leaky Gut Syndrome or intestinal permeability, which is when tiny holes are poked into the intestinal lining and the contents of the intestine spill into the bloodstream. This is the cause of many of the food allergies today.[4] This is not as uncommon as one may think since we're exposed to these pesticides on a regular basis.

BT is just one of many pesticides, and if you're eating conventional or GMO containing foods, there's a great chance you're consuming it on a daily basis. This toxin even lives in a mother's breast milk when consumed in the diet and is passed to new babies—even in the womb.[5] How is this impacting our little ones? I'm sure it's not only destroying their gut, but think about their little brains and other developing organs. Could this also be an explanation as to why children are developing so many food allergies at such a young age?

Grains and Gluten

For the most part, our grains are no longer as healthy as they were in ancient times because they are now contaminated with GMO wheat, pesticides, and are heavy carriers of mold. Gluten is a protein found in grains and is known to cause an allergic reaction in some, leading to the diagnosis of Celiac disease. Gluten protein is not an issue for all people, but many of the reactions come from the contamination of grains. Studies have found that those who follow a gluten free diet have better gut bacteria balance.[6,7] If you have Celiac disease or are sensitive to gluten, then you definitely want to avoid gluten-containing products. Many people may be able to have certain brands of sprouted wheat and grains in moderation with no problems, especially once the gut is healed. I do challenge you to remove it completely from your diet for at least one month before dismissing the fact of whether or not you have negative symptoms from it.

Although we hear about gluten, we don't hear much about the different compounds that make it up. Australian researchers have identified 400 forms of gluten that include gliadins, gluteomorphins, glutenin, lectins and wheat germ agglutinin.[8] All grains have some form of gluten. The FDA only recognizes the alpha-gliadin protein, which is only one form of gluten. If a food is alpha-gliadin free, then it can be labeled gluten free. 65% of protein in wheat is alpha-gliadin. This is why many people have such a strong reaction to wheat if they are gliadin sensitive or allergic. Rice only has five percent orzenin—another form of gluten. So you can see that neither are completely gluten free, but the FDA allows for rice to be labeled as such. Traditional gluten free is wheat, barley, and rye, but going grain free may help if you're still struggling with symptoms while following a "so-called" gluten free diet. There are several resources in the back of the book to provide more information on this subject.

Gliadin has a similar amino acid structure to that of human organs. It's what makes up the bulk of gluten and is very difficult to digest. When we develop antibodies to gliadin, our immune system begins an attack response, which can lead to autoimmunity. The fact that the compounds tested—for determining sensitivity or allergy—do not include all the compounds that make up gluten is one of the reasons that not everyone who has gluten sensitivity may show a positive reaction to it on testing. That's why it's a great idea to test all grains as part of an elimination diet to see whether or not they work for your body.

Most of our wheat is now genetically engineered, and lacks the nutrients it once carried in ancient times before heavy processing was an issue. You'll see that most grains are fortified with vitamins, which is due to the fact that the grains are stripped of naturally occurring nutrients during processing. These added nutrients are synthetic, and not naturally occurring. Manufacturers must add nutrients back in so they aren't completely void of nutrition. Grains are actually considered anti-nutrients, meaning they leach nutrients out of your body. This means you can still eat a very healthy diet, but lose many of your nutrients when you consistently consume grains. Anti-nutrients can also be found in foods like nuts and legumes. They bind to nutrients and make them unusable by the body.

This is one of the major reasons I was malnourished when I was so sick. Even though I thought I was doing the right things in the beginning by eating organic foods and taking all my supplements, I had a grain-heavy diet because that's what I enjoyed. I later learned that it was just a food addiction I had to overcome. If there's a food you must have every day and you tell yourself you can't give it up under any circumstance, then consider the fact that you may have a food addiction. I'll talk about how to overcome this addiction later.

Many people believe it's fine to eat small amounts of grains like rice, or pseudo grains like buckwheat, amaranth, and quinoa, or even ancient sprouted grains. Others believe in being strictly grain free. Pseudo grains are not true grains, but may replace them in some of our dishes to give the same textures or flavors. These alternatives have been known to cause problems in individuals with compromised guts, so test them with your own body if you want to try them as a grain replacement. If you're interested in adding grains back in after you've healed your gut, then *Eat Wheat* by John Douillard may be of interest to you. Either way, grains should not be a staple in your diet. There are too many other options that have a much higher nutrient content. Many vegans fill their plates with too many grains because they're filling. It's better to add healthy fats than to live on grains.

I will caution those of you avoiding the gliadin protein to be careful when eating rice at sushi restaurants. From my experience, as many as one-third of sushi restaurants admit to adding a scoop of flour to their sushi rice to make it sticky. If you're gluten sensitive, make sure you ask. Sashimi is a great option if you're grain free but love your raw fish fix now and then.

If you choose to include grains on a regular basis, then choose those that have been sprouted or fermented. It greatly increases the nutrient content and makes them easier to digest. Sprouting also deactivates their nutrient blockers, and will lead to less digestive problems. You can sprout seeds in your home or buy them sprouted at some grocery stores. You may have seen clover, alfalfa, broccoli, or radish sprouts, which are some of the popular ones in stores now. These have the same benefits, and actually their nutrient content is much higher than the vegetable in its full-grown state. You can add sprouts to any meal for a nutrient boost.

Remember when we're talking about grains, that includes more than just bread-like products and pasta. Another one that's often missed on a grain-free diet is corn, which is a high allergen food. It's in many processed foods in the form of cornstarch and high fructose corn syrup. Much of our corn today is genetically modified, and is included in many of the diets of our cattle and farm-raised fish to fatten them up. If it's used to fatten them up, then why would we want to consume it on a regular basis? Corn is over-produced and they're looking for things to add it to, so be careful if you're trying to avoid it. It's one of those hidden ingredients I recommend you scan for when purchasing packaged foods.

Corn and other crops are also sprayed with a pesticide known as glyphosate—developed by Monsanto—which is toxic for human consumption. They claim it's safe because it's sprayed on the plants, but we know those pesticides don't just disappear into thin air before they end up on our plate. Therefore, we are ingesting them when we eat foods that have been sprayed. Glyphosate leaches plant minerals, particularly magnesium,[9] which could explain why most people are significantly low in this mineral. It's also found in most breast milk,[10] so even when we choose the best methods for caring for our young ones, it's still difficult to escape the destruction being caused by Monsanto's greed.

Clean Protein

Many consider protein to be a "safe food." People often believe they can eat as much as desired with no ill effects. We've been informed that protein is what helps us build muscle and that it's full of amino acids and the things we need for fit-looking bodies. Experts agree you likely need about one-half gram of protein per pound of body weight for sedentary people[11] and up to one gram per pound for athletes.[12,13] Many super active athletes do take in more than that without any problems. It may also be beneficial for those looking to lose a little body fat to increase protein slightly as well.[14] I'm definitely not one to continuously measure my food, but it could work out in your favor if you have unhealthy eating habits and are looking to lose a little body fat. Keeping track for a short period of time will give you an idea about whether or not you're taking in the right amount of food energy to sustain you.

Many people are following high protein diets because of the new paleo trend. There's no single food group we should look at as the star of the show. They all play an important role in providing the body what it needs to survive and thrive. When we take in more protein than the body needs, it turns to sugar and is stored as fat. It's not very often that we hear about this little piece of "protein truth." Eating more protein than your body requires can stimulate an important biochemical pathway called the mammalian target of rapamycin (mTOR). We will not get too in depth here about what this is, but it plays an important role in many cancers. Fasting protein one day per week is beneficial because it gives this constant stimulation of mTOR a break. Maybe there is more to the "Meatless Mondays" than we thought. Meat is also acidic, as compared to vegetables. When the body is in an acidic state, cancer and other diseases can thrive more easily than if the body were alkaline.

Animals are a major source of protein for those who consume meat products. Think about the foods that conventionally-raised animals are eating today. We just discussed that many of the cattle we consume are being fed GMO corn, soy, and other grains. This is not a normal diet for them. They're eating many other foreign foods they're unable to properly digest that cause infections and disease. When these animals show signs of infection, they're pumped full of antibiotics and still processed with the other healthy animals. This is showing up more and more in the form of food recalls due to bacteria that's causing people to become ill. Another reason farmers don't want to completely go antibiotic free is because antibiotics fatten animals up and make them weigh more. They make more money on each pound of matter, whether it be meat, fat, water, or inflammation.

I spoke with a cattle rancher on a plane once and asked him about his practices. He said he could make a lot more money fattening his cattle with corn and other grains so he could sell them more quickly. He didn't seem at all concerned about health of the animals or those consuming them. He was more interested in the income his cattle were providing, even though it was not in the best interest of the animals or the people he serves. I know this is partly because of lack of education on the topic. That's why we have to take responsibility and do our own research when it comes to taking care of our bodies and what we put in them.

WE HAVE TO TAKE RESPONSIBILITY AND DO OUR OWN RESEARCH WHEN IT COMES TO TAKING CARE OF OUR BODIES

We have to be careful when choosing grass-fed meats as well. Some are grass-fed and grain-finished, while others are grain-fed and grass-finished. It's best to choose meat that's grass-fed with no grain supplementation. The labeling laws have recently changed and the USDA is no longer regulating the labeling of grass-fed meat. Purchasing chicken and eggs is difficult as well because you'll see labels that include words like "Natural," "Cage-Free," or "Humanely Raised" on their packaging. Do not fall for it. These terms are not properly regulated either.

When looking at the packaging, organic does not always mean that the animals were raised humanely, but does mean that antibiotics and GMOs were prohibited in their feed. You can also look for labels that say "Animal Welfare Approved" (AWA). These animals are typically raised humanely and have higher levels of Omega 3s naturally. You can also look for "Certified Humane" labels. I'm sure you have encountered labels from the "Global Animal Partnership," which put a number on the meat, to let consumers know how clean the meat is. Stick with those with a 4, 5, or 5+ label. You can also look for foods labeled by *American Grass-fed Association* or see that it is *Food Alliance Certified*. These are labels that let you know the animal consumed a natural diet and that it was raised and slaughtered in a humane way. You also have the option of getting to know your local farmer. Many of them will be thrilled to tell you, and even show you the condition of their livestock as well as talk to you about their feed and lifestyle.

Buying local meat has the same benefits as buying local vegetables. You can find discounts when you purchase meat in large quantities. If you don't have the space for it, then consider splitting it with a friend or family member. It's cheaper than buying grain-fed meat from grocery stores when you buy in large quantities. Many local farmers are willing to sell a cow in quarters. It sounds a little pricey initially, but is actually cheaper in the long run, especially when it comes to your family's health. If you're having a hard time finding a local farmer then you can find great meat on www.eatwild.com, and they will deliver straight to your door. Another great company to purchase meat online is US Wellness Meats. If you sign up for their updates, they send out discounts on a regular basis.

It's pretty common to see labels that say, "no hormones or antibiotics." This label is misleading as well. The conventionally raised animals you consume usually contain antibiotics—although they may not be receiving them at the time of slaughter, so they can label them as such. Many farmers are also subjecting their animals to high stress environments, especially when they are taken to slaughterhouses. They're gathered many times in inhumane ways, including rounding them up with heavy equipment. This causes the stress hormone cortisol to be released into the body of the animal. Then we consume this meat that contains high amounts of cortisol. This in turn disrupts our own hormones.

The problem with antibiotics is that we're constantly getting a low dose with each bite of conventionally raised meat we consume. With that comes "smart bugs" and antibiotic immunity. I bet everyone knows at least one person who's had an MRSA (Methicillin resistant Staphylococcus aureus) infection. This is just one of many bacteria that are now resistant to antibiotics. Bacteria are smart and they start creating different strains that are resistant to antibiotics with continuous exposure. It's their way of survival. We also see that people aren't responding to simple antibiotics in the way they used to because we've built an immunity, which leads to the need for stronger alternatives. Unfortunately, we're running out of alternatives. Of course, this is not the only cause behind smart bugs, but it is a major one. Carrying around those hand sanitizers that you constantly rub on your skin is another major issue where smart bugs are concerned.

Another important topic surrounding eating healthy meat is to watch your consumption of scavengers, or those creatures that feed on the trash of the earth. You've heard many people say, you are what you eat. Others say, you are what you digest. Some take it even one step further to say you are what you absorb. The last statement has more to do with the body's ability to properly assimilate the nutrients. The other side of that is, we're taking in everything these scavengers took in. We're filling our bodies with things that lack proper nutrients and are filled with toxic properties when we choose to consume these foods. I'm not saying we should completely avoid such things, because I know some of these creatures have benefits for the body, but filling the diet with them on a regular basis is not something I would suggest. There are many scavengers to consider, but shrimp is one of the more popular ones we see on the menu on a regular basis. Make sure you're buying wild-caught shrimp that has been responsibly harvested. You can look for the "MSC Certified" label to ensure it meets sustainability standards.

Many people are replacing meals with protein shakes. I am not against this when you're not filling your cup with sugary protein powders that have unnecessary fillers. There are many great options for both vegan protein and animal protein powders, but I encourage you to find one that's clean. I do add collagen protein to my smoothie on a regular basis. I also include things like berries, greens, superfoods, and fat of some sort. Collagen is great for the skin, hair, nails, as well as the gut and internal organs. Collagen is what's so healing in bone broth, and is a great addition to a healthy diet. If you choose whey, make sure it is from concentrate. That pretty much goes for all protein powders. Whey isolate is typically tolerated well by those who are sensitive to dairy, but the preferred method is concentrate, since isolates are much more processed. Pea protein is one of the best sources for vegans because it includes all the appropriate amino acids. I do use it on a regular basis as well.

Bone broth is a cleansing protein that's gaining popularity. You can buy it online, and have it delivered to your door in a frozen state, dehydrated powder, or you can make your own. It takes about 24-48 hours in a slow cooker or four hours in a pressure cooker. I will not give details here, but there are plenty of recipes online. I usually buy chicken feet and beef bones since I'm able to get those from a local farmer. I have ordered bones online at some of the websites I mentioned previously. I like to use both chicken and beef because although they are similar, they're superior in different ways. The beef is better for skin and joints, and the chicken is best for gut repair. If you're able to find fish bones, or can save your own, they're the best for allowing the body to naturally repair. There are times when I go on a fast for a few days that will include only bone broth. It really jump starts gut repair and is a great way to cleanse the body.

Dairy

Our dairy cows are inflamed due to a poor diet. Their milk is filled with mucus due to the fact that regulatory agencies allow certain amounts to pass into processing and consider it safe for human consumption. Researchers have found up to twenty medications lurking in our dairy products - from antibiotics and antifungals to hormones and anti-inflammatories. These could all end up in just one gallon of milk or ice cream that many people grab off the shelf and serve to their families every week. This means that even if you refuse to subject yourself to the world of pharmaceuticals, then you're still ingesting these medications and are subject to all the negative side effects they can cause. Have you listened to the commercials for a new medication lately? Sometimes the side effects are worse than the disease. It's no wonder we're feeling the effects in our bodies if we're a dumping ground for pharmaceutical companies.

Cheese and milk are highly processed. If you want to eat cheese, butter, or yogurt, then I would suggest looking for grass-fed, raw options. These are usually available at higher end grocery stores and farmers markets. Yogurt is another item that's commonly mistaken as a health food. Not only is our dairy from grain-fed cattle filled with medications and excess hormones, they are many times sick from poor living conditions. Then we add artificial sweeteners and preservatives to that and have a disease trap packaged in a nice little to-go cup for us. We're told by food companies that these are healthy breakfast or snack options. If you love your yogurt, then coconut kefir or raw milk yogurt options would be a good replacement if they have no added sugar or artificial ingredients.

Many people speak about being lactose intolerant. Pasteurization destroys the nutritional integrity of milk, making it toxic for human consumption. It also destroys the beneficial bacteria. Lactose intolerance is not an allergy or intolerance to milk. It's an inability to digest and assimilate pasteurized milk that no longer contains an enzyme known as lactase that is a necessary cofactor for processing lactose—the disaccharide sugar in milk that makes it taste sweet. Milk produced correctly from clean animals does not need to be pasteurized. Our ancestors lived on unpasteurized milk for generations. The problem lies in the fact that we're feeding them genetically modified (GM) grains, and injecting them with drugs to fatten them up. Then we allow them to wallow around in their own fecal matter rather than roam naturally in grassy pastures. This is the dairy we are consuming, and it's making us sick. If you want to consume dairy and have problems with pasteurized milk, I encourage you to try raw milk. People tend to have little issues with it when they make the switch.

Healthy Fat—Is there Such Thing?

There are many misconceptions regarding the consumption of fat. The benefits of eating this sometimes "taboo-labeled" food group have been misunderstood due to poor research. Many people still believe that fat is directly related to heart disease. Contrary to popular belief, eating fat doesn't make you fat, nor will healthy fats lead to heart disease. The culprit where heart disease is concerned is actually sugar and refined carbohydrates such as cookies, pastries, pancakes, cereals, and pastas. There's a difference between good fat and bad fat. Canola, soybean, cottonseed, corn, safflower, and sunflower oil are popular cooking oils we should avoid. These oils are generally heavily processed, highly GM, and are related to cardiovascular and autoimmune disease, cancer, vitamin E deficiency, and liver damage to name a few. These oils are heated to high temperatures during processing, which causes them to go rancid quickly. Questionable chemicals are also introduced into these oils, which we end up ingesting.

Years ago, I remember thinking that fat was the enemy. I would avoid it because I thought it would make me fat. After all, that was the trend, and supposedly the verdict of the latest and greatest research. I ate low fat dressings, mayonnaise, yogurt, cheese, milk, and the list goes on. Removing the fat removes a lot of the flavor, so companies have to replace the flavor with other preservatives or sweeteners to make up for it. These low fat options are much worse for us than their full fat cousins.

As I began to learn the truth about fat, I quickly realized the benefits. Some of the things I noticed in my own life when I started eating a higher fat diet was a reduction in brain fog, feeling satiated for longer periods of time, better regulated blood glucose, and more energy. Before this change, I always had to have a snack on hand in case I had a drop in blood sugar. The word "hangry" was definitely a word I used on a frequent basis to describe how I felt when it was time for my next meal or snack. We've all been there—so hungry that we don't hesitate biting someone's head off before we even think about the fact that our hunger has caused this major mood swing. The truth is, fat is the only macronutrient that has little impact on blood sugar levels, where carbohydrates and proteins can both cause an increase in blood sugars. Increase in blood sugar is what causes increase in fat storage in the fat cells. So it's not fat that makes us fat after all.

When I was diagnosed with hypoglycemia at age 7, I'm almost certain they never discussed the importance of not only avoiding sugar, but consuming extra fat to help control blood sugar for longer periods of time. It's true that fat was not looked upon in a positive light back then. Even now, most doctors receive so little education on the importance of diet that the likelihood of them having this knowledge today is very slim unless they've researched the topic on their own.

Without fat, we can't absorb fat soluble vitamins, like A, D, E and K. With a greater understanding of the topic, it makes sense that so many people are malnourished. Not only because they're not consuming nutrient-filled vegetables, but also because they may not have the appropriate amount of fat to absorb those nutrients.

One other little tip I'll include about fat is its satiating abilities. I start my day with a breakfast full of fat and I'm sure to make it to lunch or after with no thought of a snack. I fill my vegetables with plenty of healthy fats, and a side of protein and have no desire to eat for hours. I've also been known to eat a whole avocado with lunch or Dinner. If I have meat protein for lunch with these fat-filled vegetables and an avocado, then there are many times I will not even be hungry for dinner. On those nights, I prepare a mixture of cooked and raw plant foods with a side of fermented vegetables and I am completely satisfied. I do like to eat my larger meal at night, but do what works best for you. It may prevent you from snacking during the day. Determining whether or not your heaviest meal gives you a boost of energy or provides comfort to wind down will help you decide the best time to have it. If you find that you're sleepy after lunch, then it may be that you're not eating the right foods and it shows because your food is not serving you. Spikes in blood sugar with a big drop are a likely cause of this afternoon lag.

Healthy fats include those like coconut oil, avocado, raw nuts and seeds, grass-fed butter, and organic egg yolks. Avoid oils that say they're refined or hydrogenated even partially-hydrogenated as these are highly processed. When purchasing oils, choose unrefined versions. Cold-pressed extra virgin is the purest form of oil you can buy. Since there has been an increased popularity in the use of olive oil, much of it has been adulterated. Tom Mueller has a passion for making sure low-grade olive oils are not passed off as "pure" or "extra-virgin" when they're not. TheTruthInOliveOil.com is a place where consumers can find answers to their olive oil concerns as well as advice about buying and enjoying oil. He lists the best options on the site. When you find a good one, you'll taste the difference.

Olive oil becomes toxic when heated to high temperatures. You can slightly warm it, but especially when using extra-virgin olive oil, use it only in cold or room temperature meals like homemade dressings and such. Seed oils are linked to higher rates of inflammation and problems with insulin and leptin. Eat seeds, not seed oils. Avocado is one of my favorites, especially for improving collagen. It tends to oxidize easily, so be gentle when applying heat to it. Coconut oil is a good choice for cooking at high temperatures, and adds a nice sweet flavor. Grass-fed Ghee (clarified butter) is another great high-heat option for those who like butter but don't tolerate casein or lactose. You can find ghee in the grocery and health food stores, but be careful as much of is not grass-fed. It's definitely one of the foods I find easier to purchase online.

I use a company called Thrive Market for online shopping. It's an online discount store with healthier options for packaged items. They do sell ghee, as well as a few other fats I enjoy, like grass-fed lard, chia seed, hemp seed, nuts and raw cacao. Chia and hemp can be added to almost anything for added fat and nutrients. They're also a great source of Omega 3's. The benefits of chia and flax seeds are greater if they're ground. These two seeds will also thicken up soups or smoothies. When buying nuts and seeds, opt for sprouted versions when possible, or at least to mix things up. When sprouted, the phytic acid is broken down and they become more bioavailable and easier to digest. This also increases their pH, which can assist the body in becoming more alkaline, where disease is less likely to thrive.

Nuts are also high in omega 3s. Watch your intake because they also have a high amount of omega 6s, which will lead to inflammation in the body. Many nuts are also very high in carbohydrates. There was a time I ate them freely because I viewed them as a healthy snack option. It's very easy to mindlessly eat too many since they're bite sized and have that sweet crunch that many of us find addictive. I found it very easy to go through a 12 ounce bag of cashews or macadamia nuts in a day, or a jar of peanut butter in 2 days.

Peanuts are often mistaken as a nut, but they are in the legume family. If you have problems with legumes, then you may find avoiding peanuts to prove beneficial. Peanuts also have a high mold content. They can be a major source of inflammation and lead to adverse symptoms. I thought I could never give up peanut butter, but found it to be a game changer once I did. Peanuts are high in fat though. If you are looking for a creamy replacement, then I recommend Barney Butter "Smooth Almond Butter." It's raw, blanched almonds (skins removed), ground into a creamy nut butter that reminds me so much of peanut butter. Most people who don't like almond butter actually love this because it's not gritty and removes a lot of the acid that the skins carry.

Speaking of my unhealthy love for peanuts, if you find a food addicting then you probably should not keep it in your house—no matter how healthy it is. I realized that mindlessly eating nuts was a major source of inflammation for me. I know others who eat them with no problem. You have to listen to your own body's needs when it comes to things like that. It sometimes takes a little experimentation to find what works best for your body.

> IF YOU FIND A FOOD ADDICTING THEN YOU PROBABLY SHOULD NOT KEEP IT IN YOUR HOUSE

Another great high-fat food source is salmon. It's also loaded with Omega 3s. This particular fat has a positive impact on almost every organ system. When choosing salmon, make sure it's wild caught. Farm raised fish is fed corn and soy, and is full of antibiotics and pesticides. This disrupts their fatty acid profile, which has to do with the amount of Omega 3 in relation to Omega 6. Just know that you want to consume higher amounts of Omega 3 for less inflammation in the body.

Alaska is the only state that does not allow farm raised fish, so you'll find waters that are less contaminated, therefore have cleaner fish. I'll also caution you about your tilapia intake, since it's very trendy right now. Tilapia is one of the most contaminated fish, full of pesticides, and farm-raised at higher rates than any other. Make sure you're purchasing wild caught fish for the healthiest option.

Carbohydrates—Should We Avoid Them?

Cutting back on carbohydrates and sugars will eliminate the need to eat so often. The constant hunger that comes with consuming high amounts of carbohydrates happens because blood sugar levels are not regulated as they should be. When we consume too many of the foods that turn to sugar in the body—in the form of starchy carbs or sugary snacks—our bodies become accustomed to burning sugar for fuel instead of fat. Both can be used for energy, but if we consume the right foods then we can teach the body to use its fat stores for fuel instead of sugar.

Living a high carbohydrate lifestyle leads you through a vicious cycle that makes it almost impossible to lose excess body fat. The fuel your body needs is coming from the sugars instead of fat, and when those stores are depleted, it signals to the body that you're hungry. You then take in more of your typical high carbohydrate foods to last another couple of hours. If you learn to replace those foods with fat, the body will begin to see fat as its energy source and when it burns all the fat from the food, then it will begin to burn fat from the body. This will keep you satiated for longer periods of time as well as help you rid the body of excess fat. We should not feel the need to eat every couple of hours due to hunger. Once we balance the blood sugar, that need will go away.

Low carbohydrate diets are one of the latest fads. Food companies are marketing low carb chips and processed junk and people buy it simply because they're following a low carb diet. There are a few things I want to bring into the light regarding carbs. Number one, they are not the enemy. We need to realize that we have to find the proper combination of carbs, fats, and proteins that work for our individual bodies. Carbohydrates are an immediate source of energy. There are different types of carbohydrates, so they cannot be lumped into one category and share the classification, with all carbs being labeled as healthy or unhealthy, just like the fats we previously discussed.

Vegetables and fruits are complex carbohydrates. They increase our glucose levels in a natural healthy way. This provides our body with an immediate source of energy. Within vegetables, we have starchy and non-starchy varieties. Non-starchy vegetables include leafy greens, asparagus, broccoli, cauliflower, cucumbers, mushrooms, onions, peppers, and the like. At least half of your meal should include these types of vegetables—and you can eat them until you are full. Some of these, especially greens and those in the cruciferous family can have a bitter taste if you are not used to eating them. Add them sparingly to other dishes to get used to the taste. Your body will thank you and you'll eventually begin to crave them.

Sunlight is accumulated in plants as they grow. We get to take in that energy when we consume them. This is also where we receive chlorophyll—from the green plants. It has the same job for plants as our blood has for our bodies. It allows us to capture the sunlight from the plant and helps keep oxidative stress down in the body. We receive great energy and vitality by eating living foods.

Starchy vegetables include squash, carrots, parsnips, potatoes, yams, and peas. You may notice they have a sweeter taste, because of their higher sugar content. Most people should eat these a little more sparingly than non-starchy vegetables. They're also more difficult to digest with a high protein meal for some individuals. If you are a steak and potatoes guy or gal, then you may want to pay attention to how you feel after this type meal. Your body will tell you whether or not it can handle it.

Meals should give you energy, not make you feel bloated or tired. Many people believe they have to experience a lag in energy after lunch. This is simply not true if you consume foods that serve you. Root vegetables are beneficial because they have a lot of fiber, which also adds bulk to your stool. If you're increasing your vegetable intake, do it slowly if you notice gastrointestinal upset. The extra fiber can be a little harsh to begin with if you change your diet too quickly.

Personally, I cut bread, pasta, and other products containing wheat and grains (including corn) from my diet. These are known as simple carbohydrates. I know this is a controversial topic, so I cannot say this will work for everyone, but it was a life-changer for me. As I mentioned earlier in our grain discussion, I challenge you to cut these foods from your diet for a period of at least one month and introduce them back in to see how you feel. You may feel so good you decide not to reintroduce them. Those who have unexplained brain fog, joint pain, inflammation, abdominal bloating and pain, decreased circulation, or daytime sleepiness may benefit from this challenge. If you want to cut simple carbohydrate intake, cutting grains is one of the most effective ways. This will get you very close to the ultimate goal of a diet that constitutes mostly whole foods.

The casein protein found in dairy products is closely related to gluten, which is found in much of our grains. Many who are sensitive to gluten protein are also sensitive to casein protein in dairy. If you know or suspect you have a gluten sensitivity then cut dairy during that period as well and introduce those food groups one at a time at least ten days apart to see if you can tell a difference in the way you feel. Another common plant culprit worth mentioning is nightshades. These are foods like tomatoes, eggplant, and peppers. If you do an elimination diet then this is another food group worth testing since there's a large part of the population with intolerances to these foods.

Keep in mind that allergies and food sensitivities are different. You'll usually show immediate symptoms with allergies, but food sensitivities can be delayed. Take this into consideration when reintroducing multiple foods so you don't introduce them too close together. Listen to your body. If you have adverse symptoms when you reintroduce the foods then do your best to avoid them in the future. Heart rate tends to increase by about 17 beats per minute with suspect foods. Measuring the heart rate before and several times after eating a suspect food is a good way to test. If there's an increase then you may have found an offender. There are apps you can download on your phone to assist with this too.

Fruit is a healthy snack option if you find it necessary to snack, but most people are consuming too much. We've gone crazy over fruit smoothies and adding fruit to breakfast plates as well as lunch or dinner salads. Fruit contains fructose, which is a sugar that is stored as fat. Although fruit does contain fiber, our fruit today contains much more sugar and is a lot larger in size than the fruit our ancestors ate. Adding a little fruit to smoothies is a great healthy option, but make sure you're not over-indulging, and opt for berries and citrus varieties, which contain less sugar. You can also squeeze a little lemon or lime in your smoothie for added flavor and to make it more alkaline. Citrus also gives smoothies a nice flavor punch. A good rule of thumb I like to use for smoothies is to have four times more vegetables than fruit. I'm not opposed to fruit, but high amounts could be a hindrance if weight loss is your goal.

If you're adding protein powders to your fruit smoothies, I would be careful about adding fruit to any of your smoothies that contain grains, like oatmeal or rice. When grains are consumed at the same time as fruit, it can cause the fruit to ferment in the gut and can cause gas and bloating and could lead to late morning fatigue. While you may want to have a breakfast smoothie, be careful when choosing your ingredients. Test this for yourself to see how you feel. If it causes digestive upset for you, there are plenty of other healthy options for protein powders when you want to use fruit in combination - whey or collagen being two.

Sugar—Satan's Legal "Substance of Choice"

Oh the temptations that come with sugar addiction. I know how real this is because I've been there, and my heart hurts for those who are experiencing this now. You can overcome this addiction! My journey has been a long one, but it has been conquered. From a girl who could eat a large, icing-filled cookie in less than 24 hours to no sugar cravings at all, I know you can do it too. I'm not talking about a big cookie, I mean the *Big* "happy birthday" style ones that you get from the bakery. At one point in my life, one bite led to half the cookie, and before I knew it the whole thing. I felt like my body craved it, and I didn't care how it tasted sometimes. I just needed to devour the sugar. This was a major source of my malnourishment, and today I'm free from that.

> *"Those who belong to Christ Jesus have crucified the flesh with its passions and desires."*
>
> GALATIANS 5:24 NIV

I could talk for days about sugar. I was the one with a sweet tooth that could not be quenched. I ate ice cream and brownies, sometimes three times a day. If I wanted chocolate covered peanuts then I would buy a pound and eat the whole thing! Once I took that first bite of sugar, it's all I wanted for the rest of the day. I didn't care if I ate real food. I would reason in my mind that I could consume fewer calories at dinner if I just skipped the meal and went straight for dessert, because there was no way I was giving up my chocolate cake.

I was so addicted to sugar and processed junk that even when I started on my path to wellness, I still remained sick because of my sugar intake. I exchanged preservative and chemical filled sweets for organic ones, thinking I was doing my body a favor. Don't get me wrong—if I decide to have a treat today, I do go for the organic ones with ingredients I can pronounce. But sugar should not be the bulk of our diet, organic or not. These are called treats for a reason. They should be consumed sparingly. That white, processed sugar and flour so many put in their bodies daily is a major source of disease.

Research shows that sugar is as addictive as heroin. In one study, when rats were given the option to choose sugar or cocaine, they chose the sugar.[15] There have been several studies that show the reward behavior associated with consuming a high fat/sugar food like Oreo® cookies elicits an equal reward response as cocaine and morphine. Food companies are smart, and they want you to crave their products. Look at the labels on the items you purchase most. You may be shocked to find that many of them are filled with sugar. Anything from spaghetti sauce to canned vegetables have added sugar. As a matter of fact, over half of our canned foods contain added sugar. Read your food labels. Every four grams of sugar is equal to one teaspoon. So imagine pouring a whole teaspoon of sugar or more over your plate of spaghetti. That's essentially what you're doing when you eat those canned sauces with added sugars.

There are many sugar alternatives, and some are better than others. Do you think you're safe with those no calorie or low calorie sweeteners? If so, think again. One study found that when given the option between water sweetened with saccharin and intravenous cocaine, 94 percent of animals chose the sweet taste of saccharin.[16] I would stay away from most sugar alternatives, including saccharin, Splenda®, and Equal®. This is what's in your "oh so healthy" yogurt and diet soda. Stay away from these. Just because they say no calorie or low calorie doesn't mean they're healthy. We need to train our brains to focus on and start counting chemicals instead of calories. Corn syrup and agave are also unhealthy options. We've discussed the problems with corn, but agave is just another high fructose sweetener that's stored as fat. The great marketing has most believing it's a healthy option.

COUNT THE CHEMICALS INSTEAD OF COUNTING THE CALORIES

Local honey, maple syrup, and coconut sugar are good options as they are not as heavily processed. Another category of alternatives include whole leaf stevia and monk fruit. These are some of the best options, but you *must* be careful about additives and preservatives in certain brands. Again, read the labels to make sure you are purchasing pure products. I find that mixing some of the healthier options is best, depending on what I am making. For example, if you find that stevia is a little bitter, you can add xylitol or erythritol to balance the taste. Both are a little less sweet than sugar, but are granulated about the same. You can add the same amount of these sugar alcohols to a recipe in place of sugar with a little stevia and get a similar result. Just play around to find what you like best. There are also recipes online to help guide you with the conversion.

I'll caution you with sugar alcohols like xylitol in particular, but erythritol as well. They can cause digestive upset if you consume too much. If you make the mistake of overeating it then it will be a gentle reminder that moderation is the key. If you use xylitol, make sure it's from birch and not corn, especially if you plan to avoid grains and GMOs. There is controversy with this sweetener because some say it disrupts the gut microflora, but it will likely not cause problems if it's consumed on occasion. When choosing stevia, make sure you choose whole leaf stevia instead of stevia extract, which goes through a chemical laden process. If you prefer liquid stevia, there is a dark liquid stevia that's made with the whole leaf.

Sugar addicts must use an "all or nothing" approach when eliminating sugar. Very few can eat it sparingly, especially when addiction is an issue. If you're a heroin addict, you cannot just have a little heroin every now and then. I don't recommend using sugar alternatives at all until you have your addiction under control. For some people, that may mean never. How do you know when your addiction is under control? When you can have a sweet treat and not crave sugar afterward, or when you can have a meal and not crave something sweet after. When you are at the point when you don't crave sugar then you can safely try the alternatives. Until then, I would remain strict with a sugar free diet—even sugary fruits. Some brains are just wired in a way that it's best to remove it completely to avoid temptation to overindulge.

When you're eating nutrient dense foods, healthy fats, and getting the appropriate daily intake of vitamins and minerals, you'll notice your cravings start to diminish greatly. When I first realized this, I would take a shot of liquid minerals every time I had a sugar craving, and it usually went away. I remember loving chocolate as much as I loved my husband, but when I regulated my magnesium levels, my chocolate cravings went away. Now I can enjoy the fruity treats as much as the creamy chocolate. Chocolate cravings can also surface when we need love. Your body will tell you what it needs. You just have to learn to look for the cause of your craving. When it hits, look within yourself and ask what's going on. It could guide you to your solution. Getting to the root, whether it be emotional or physical is key.

Nature's Flavor

One of the main reasons people find the thought of a whole foods diet unappealing is due to the inaccurate belief that it lacks flavor. Giving up flavorful sauces and eating plain raw or steamed vegetables can seem unappealing, but it's not a necessary swap when you're adding in more of these plant foods. For example, you can still have your creamy dishes if you choose to remove dairy. You will just learn to use avocado, coconut milk, or cashews for making homemade dressings and sauces.

Using spices is another way to bring additional flavor to a dish. Use the same caution when choosing spices as you do with produce. Organic is always best. If you're just getting started, stick with blends until you learn more about spices you like. You can buy taco, Italian, Cajun, or try different blends that can be added to any vegetable dish. Buy spices in quantities small enough that you will use it in about 6 months. Many times, I'll buy single spices and make my own blends from recipes I find online. We're likely all guilty of keeping our spices too long. If you have spices in your cabinet that are several years old, throw them out. They not only lose their potency, but they're a good place for unseen mold or bacteria to settle. When we season our food as it's cooking, steam rises and moisture builds up in the spice jar, which can be the perfect place for mold to grow once we put it back in our dark cabinet. It's a great habit to remove the lid entirely and pour it in your hand instead.

Salt is feared by many, especially those with hypertension or other heart diseases. Table salt (sodium chloride) is actually stripped of its nutritional value due to heavy processing, and you're correct if you believe it has a negative impact on your health. It's one seasoning you should fear. On the other hand, when you choose Himalayan or Celtic sea salt, you'll reap the benefits from the wonderful minerals they provide. These salts don't cause a rise in blood pressure or lead to further disease processes. They actually help with hydration, improve electrolyte imbalance, and are beneficial to the adrenal and thyroid hormones, among others—even if you have high cholesterol. We discussed that earlier, but if you happen to have high cholesterol, consider ditching the breads and sugars and adding some sea salt before ditching salt altogether. Your labs will tell you the truth.

"Those who have no time for healthy eating will sooner or later have to find time for illness."

EDWARD STANLEY

C H A P T E R   F O U R

Alternative Therapies

Healing Practices Forgotten by Western Medicine

If we looked at healthcare from a preventative standpoint rather than a tertiary one, we would likely not suffer from sickness and disease in our latter years. We could live well past 100 years in divine health.

> *Then the LORD Said, "My Spirit shall not strive with man forever, because he also is flesh; nevertheless his days shall be one hundred and twenty years."*
>
> GENESIS 6:3 (NASB)

Do you see that? Should normal healthy people not be able to live 120 years? Jesus already bore all our sickness and disease on the cross, so we should live in divine health until this age. This should occur without degenerative disease, neurological problems, joint pain, or anything else that most people associate with aging. We should all age gracefully. Hallelujah! However, this is dependent on what you choose to believe and how you choose to treat your body.

I believe there's a time and place for conventional medicine. Medical professionals are doing as they are trained, but imagine if they teamed up with our Creator where healing the sick is concerned. What a different world we would have. What if all people had the faith and understanding of God as our healer? We would only depend on medicine for emergencies, a diagnosis, and necessary surgeries as God used those men and women in their areas of expertise. We wouldn't need medicine for every ailment we experienced. We would instead call on our Heavenly Father who is ready and willing to heal. Healing is ours for the taking.

The world we live in today is toxic. Our food system is polluted with pesticides and hormones, and is being genetically engineered. The air we breathe and the water we drink and bathe in is a dumping ground for anything from pharmaceuticals to heavy metals and chemicals. We need antioxidants now more than ever. Contradicting research and viewpoints leave many uncertain about how to wrap their heads around it all.

I've learned that you must be very careful as to whose research you're listening to. First, make sure you look at who is funding the study. When you're reading a study funded by a soda company that concludes diet soda helps people lose weight, then consider the fact that they're likely just promoting their product. Everyone has a hypothesis going into a research study, otherwise there would be no need for the study. It's important to consider the source when we're sifting through the plethora of information we are constantly flooded with. If we're not careful, our reading could lead us to taking a cabinet full of supplements with no real results. The goal should be to get to the root of the issue and resolve from there.

There are many types of preventative care therapies. One that we've already covered is a healthy diet. I'll outline some of the ones here that I feel have been beneficial in my own healing journey. This list is not all-inclusive, but some of my favorites are colon hydrotherapy, supplementation, and the use of essential oils. We'll also discuss the importance of detoxing, sweating, and moving our bodies a bit later as well.

Supplementation

I'll never forget the time I had a conversation with a guy who told me his doctor didn't believe in supplementation (as I was popping a handful of vitamins at the lunch table). He said if you need vitamin C then just eat an orange. I thought to myself, "Well your doctor doesn't even know that bell peppers have more vitamin C than an orange?" Of course, everyone really doesn't know that, but it's true. It was just something I had chosen to educate myself on. The truth is, most of us don't know what to eat to provide our bodies with a wide range of nutrients, and even if we did, our food is still lacking the things we need. One easy tip to remember is to eat a wide variety and eat the rainbow. That will give you the best chance of consuming the necessary vitamins and minerals to thrive.

As we touched on briefly with our sugar discussion, you can probably see that minerals are pretty important. The bacteria in our soil helps bring balance to our gut health. These bacteria that should be present have been degraded because of persistent chemical pollution in the form of pesticides and herbicides. Our soils are depleted of minerals and are never replenished. This means we're eating foods that are empty of nutrients. People often ask why we need to supplement if our food is supposed to nourish us. While it does provide nourishment, it's a lot less than what our ancestors received from it. We also don't eat a wide variety of foods to give us the range of nutrients we need. Another cause of nutrient depletion is that our food travels long distances before it ends up on our plate. It's picked early, so it's lacking in nutrients it otherwise would have if we picked it ripe. It's important for gardeners to remember to add minerals back into the soil, which is not a common practice.

I won't go into detail about many of the supplements I use, although I do take a handful every day. I will tell you that my favorite multivitamin supplement includes both vitamins and minerals. Although it's not something I take daily, it is one I keep on hand to add in when my diet needs a little more nutritional support. I also rotate between a few green powders, spirulina and chlorella, and other similar supplements on top of a healthy diet. Be careful which brands you use. They're not all created equal and you do get what you pay for with supplements. Look at the ingredients. If you're gluten sensitive, you may want to watch for symptoms when drinking green powders that contain different "grasses" because depending on when they're harvested, they could have gluten proteins. Many can be sensitive to those as well, so test them and listen to your body.

In order to get a range of benefits from my supplements, I like to rotate between them monthly, weekly, or even daily. I do this with different probiotics, fish oils, digestive enzymes, and antioxidants. There is one glutathione supplement I love because it's made the greatest difference in my blood tests after taking it. It's called RegActiv. Glutathione is one of the master antioxidants. I do not take this supplement all the time, but it's in my rotation. You'll notice that I don't recommend many different brands, but this is one I really do believe in. Antioxidants all have different benefits. One of my other favorite superfood antioxidants is Ganoderma Lucidum, better known as the reishi mushroom. I do like others in the mushroom family as well and use lion's mane, cordyceps, chaga, and a few others on a regular basis.

When I first started seeing a functional medicine doctor, my gallbladder was only functioning at 40%. I would have severe attacks but I never told anyone about it because I knew they would want to remove it. My doctor agreed to watch it but did nothing to help with ideas about how to heal it. I learned then that all functional medicine doctors are not created equal. We still have to educate ourselves and take responsibility for our own health. It was at that point that I took it upon myself to research supplements that would improve the health of my liver and gallbladder. I started taking things like phyllanthus, artichoke, glutathione, dandelion root tea, and desiccated liver.

The liver can become taxed when gallbladder disease is present because it has to produce bile on demand. It took a little over a year to get to a point where I didn't have gallbladder attacks, but I now can vouch for the power of supplementation. Attacks occurred less and less often, until I felt supplementation was no longer necessary. Today I no longer take anything for my gallbladder, and have been symptom free for years, even when eating high amounts of fat. I remember those painful attacks that would even come with eating too many nuts. Now I have a diet full of healthy fats that make up a large percentage of my total daily calories. I do still enjoy my dandelion tea some mornings as well as digestive enzymes with meals to assist with proper digestion.

Vitamin D and magnesium are two nutrients that most people are deficient in. Proper vitamin D levels can help reduce the risk of common diseases like Alzheimer's, diabetes, chronic inflammation, and macular degeneration. It can also help fight infections like the common cold, flu and pneumonia. Sun exposure can help increase the levels of vitamin D, but supplementation is needed in a large percentage of those tested to reach optimal levels.

Magnesium works synergistically with vitamin D, as well as vitamin k2 and calcium. Magnesium is used mainly by your heart, kidneys, and muscles, but is used by every organ in the body. Fatigue, muscle spasms, abnormal heart rhythms, nausea, numbness and tingling are some of the early symptoms of deficiency.[1] Magnesium comes in many different forms, but one you may find fun is magnesium sulphate, which is in Epsom salts. You can add it to your bathwater and soak for absorption through the skin. Many people also find more restful sleep when they have sufficient magnesium levels. Try your warm Epsom salt bath at night before bed and I'm sure you'll notice a difference in how well you rest.

The best way to decide what your body needs is to do a nutrition panel. I would suggest doing this several times a year. As your diet changes, so will your nutritional needs. It won't hurt to begin taking a multivitamin and mineral supplement as you start making changes to your lifestyle. There are many great multivitamins available, so I encourage you to explore them and find the one that is best for you. You can adjust and add other specific nutrients you need depending on your lab results. Yes, I'm one of those with the expensive urine! Call it what you want, but I'd rather pay now for expensive urine and organic groceries and live in health than pay later in medical bills and die sick.

Most people focus on vitamins when they are looking to supplement. Mineral deficiency has been linked to most diseases though. As I studied the topic, I learned that almost any disease state can be prevented with proper mineral intake. It's rare to get them in proper doses from food, so I choose to supplement. Again, it's super important that you take quality supplements. For example, some calcium supplements in stores are ground up calcium rocks and they're not digestible by the body. So even with supplements, you must use the best or else you could be doing more harm than

MINERAL SUPPLEMENTS ARE AS IMPORTANT AS VITAMINS, TAKING QUALITY SUPPLEMENTS IS KEY good. Some of the ones I like are in the back of the book. There are many others, but I've chosen to stick to listing those who analyze the contents of their compounds on a regular basis and go through third party testing. That doesn't mean these are the only good supplements that exist. You can also look to some of the resources and their recommendations or consult with a functional medicine doctor to see what brands they recommend.

Again, quality supplementation is key. I worked for years to get my magnesium levels into an optimal range. I tried different brands, different types, different doses, and nothing worked. I was changing something in my regimen and testing every couple months for several years with little to no improvement. I did go through an extreme detox program and always took reputable supplement brands, but finally switched to the Metagenics magnesium citrate. I cannot say that particular brand or type will work for everyone, but it was the golden ticket for me. I know Metagenics is a pharmaceutical grade supplement and they go through strict testing to make sure they're including everything the label says they are. Quality supplements can be a little more expensive, but why pay anything for a pill that's going to end up in the toilet in its whole form because your body did nothing to break it down? So, I say pay the price for the good stuff, test your levels, and use what works for you.

Food Addiction

If you find you're craving a particular food all the time, you could have some type of deficiency that's causing you to do so—or it could be addiction. Sometimes addictions and allergies go hand in hand. When your body starts running low on the food you're addicted to, you start to crave it. At the point of that craving, start asking yourself questions. Am I really hungry? Many times we don't know the difference between physical hunger and our emotional desire to eat. You can even experience cravings as physical hunger, meaning your stomach could growl to tell you it's time to eat. It may take training yourself to learn the difference. Other questions to ask yourself are: "How will I feel once I eat this food? Will I be able to stop after I have a taste, or will it lead to additional cravings? Would something else satisfy me right now, or will only this buttery yeast roll do the trick?" Your answers can help you determine whether it's true hunger.

When we become dependent on a food, withdrawals may come in the form of hunger or cravings for that specific food. We feel good when we eat it, and the cycle continues. We must eat this addictive food on a regular basis to avoid withdrawal symptoms. Many times we just shove those foods in without even tasting them because our body needs them to feed the unhealthy bacteria we've created in our gut. They need those foods to survive. We don't look at hunger as a withdrawal symptom, but it very well can be.

The best way to get rid of unhealthy food addiction is to remove all temptations, get through the moment, and avoid that food, period! Keep it out of the house and don't go places where you'll be tempted to eat it. You can't place a beer in front of an alcoholic and tell him not to drink. The same is true for a sugar addict. If the smell of the cookie shop is too irresistible to avoid when going to the mall, then shop online until that desire has faded. A great resource for overcoming food addiction is Teresa Shields Parker. She has overcome a serious food addiction and has helped thousands of others do the same. I encourage you to look into her work if you're facing this issue. She has several great books on the topic, one of which is *Sweet Grace: How I Lost 250 Pounds and Stopped Trying to Earn God's Favor.* She'll teach you how to get to the root of your addiction so you can overcome it.

I know removing addictive foods from your diet is very difficult because I have been there, but after a while, you will likely forget how much you once loved them. I was addicted to processed cheese and bread, but now I don't even care for them after removing them from my diet for so long. I remember needing those foods. If you feel there is a food you're unable to give up then you're likely addicted to it. The best way to break the addiction is to stop cold-turkey. Just eliminate it from your diet for good.

I did many elimination periods for twenty-eight days and never found relief from the addiction of sugar. The minute my twenty-eight days ended, the food would sneak back in and negative symptoms would come back with a vengeance.

When I realized I couldn't do it on my own, I partnered with God for assistance. The instructions He gave me were shocking. I learned that giving up certain foods was impossible because they were idols. When He revealed this to me, I couldn't believe it. It didn't make sense. Then the revelation came that anything we hold onto and are not willing to release is technically a form of an idol, because we are putting it on a pedestal. The Father will not compete with anything else.

I was already living a lifestyle of fasting. Anytime I felt like there was something carnal in the way of my relationship with the Lord, He would call me to a fast and instruct me with what I needed to give up and for how long. These lasted anywhere from one day to three or four weeks. There were a few different food groups that I usually fasted, but it was because I kept bringing those back into my diet in excess when the fast was complete.

One day, He told me to fast a few certain foods for forty days. These were those food groups I was experiencing addictive tendencies toward. After learning that I was crucifying the flesh and truly giving it to Him to handle, my fast was super easy. I actually decided to do it for fifty days instead and experienced freedom like never before. I have absolutely no food cravings today. There are still foods I avoid for the most part, but if I want to have a treat, then I do so without feeling guilty. It's a treat, not a cheat. He showed me that freedom was possible. When I gave up trying to do it myself and released it, He made it possible. He doesn't mind if we have fun foods now and then, but it becomes a problem when we feel we can't live without them.

> WHEN I GAVE UP TRYING TO DO IT MYSELF AND RELEASED IT, HE MADE IT POSSIBLE

If addiction to a certain food is an issue, then all or nothing may be the best solution. If not, you may see those foods creep back in and take control. It's a great idea to work with a health coach to teach you how to get through the tough times.

Food Allergy, Intolerance, or Sensitivity

We briefly discussed allergies a little earlier when talking about how to clean up the diet. They are worth mentioning again because they're one aspect of health that's often overlooked for years when a patient is being seen by a conventional medicine doctor. I had medical problems from my childhood and saw many practitioners who never mentioned the possibility of allergies or food sensitivities. I finally took it upon myself to have them tested after researching my symptoms and eliminating foods with no sign of relief. Sometimes an elimination diet will work, but if there's no relief after removing common culprits, it's best to test. The foods we often crave the most are many times the ones we have allergies to.

With true allergies, you tend to get an immediate negative response. Sometimes intolerances and food sensitivities cause a delayed response, so it's difficult to tell what may be causing the reaction. This delay could often appear up to three weeks after the exposure. Either way, if it's a sensitivity, intolerance or allergy, the food should be avoided. If you're eating a problematic food on a regular basis then you'll likely get used to the symptoms, or possibly overlook them. The food is still adding chronic stress to the body, even though it doesn't appear to be a major issue.

After cleaning up the gut, we can begin to reintroduce them and will many times see that after some time, they are non-issues. I know that's been the case for me, and I've seen it happen with others as well.

Gut Health

Many of us have either received the diagnosis or know someone who suffers from IBS (Irritable Bowel Syndrome), which is many times accompanied by disabling symptoms of bloating, diarrhea, constipation, and pain. This gastrointestinal upset experienced by many people today is known as "Leaky Gut Syndrome" or "Intestinal Permeability" in the world of functional medicine. The name really does explain the disorder. We briefly touched on leaky gut when we discussed the toxins that our foods are coated with, which can lead to a compromised gut. It makes sense that many of us live with constant symptoms, now that we understand what's going on inside our body. Although there are many culprits, the main causes of leaky gut are food allergies from a poor diet, overgrowth of bacteria in the small intestine, stress, and toxic burden on the body.

YOU DON'T HAVE TO LIVE WITH SYMPTOMS OF A LEAKY GUT—THESE CAN BE ADDRESSED AT THEIR ROOT AND ELIMINATED

Dr. Josh Axe has a beautiful understanding of the subject of gut health, and much of his work is freely accessible online. He has a program that provides individuals with the steps to heal their gut, without the use of unnecessary medications and surgeries that don't usually help in the long-run anyway. In short, when the gut becomes compromised and tiny food particles begin to escape into the bloodstream, it puts the body in attack mode. This is a natural fight response that protects us against foreign invaders. These food particles are treated as foreign invaders by the body—basically because they are floating around in areas they don't belong. When we continue to ingest them, our symptoms become worse, and the gut lining is in a constant state of irritation. This inflammatory response to these food particles has a negative impact on every organ system of the body since these particles are being carried throughout the blood as they are simultaneously being attacked.

Removing inflammatory food is a must to completely heal the gut. Once you free your diet from culprit foods, you'll likely almost immediately notice negative symptoms when you're exposed. It's a great reminder of what a negative impact foods can have on your ability to function optimally. You'll then have to decide if you're willing to compromise in those areas. It's a lot of trial and error if you decide to reintroduce culprit foods, but you'll quickly realize what your own body will allow in moderation and what you must completely eliminate. Making dietary changes to put the gut microbiome in a healthy state is key.

Repairing gut imbalances is dependent on the cause. There are tests your physician can do to find out if you have bacterial overgrowth or fungal infections. There are also tests for allergies and other culprits that lead to a compromised gut. Many times more than one is present, and the treatment will depend heavily on the reason for illness. Cleaning up the diet and focusing on colorful, live plant foods with moderate intake of meat and removing sugar, alcohol, and processed foods is a great place to start. It's also a good idea to reduce stress, exercise regularly, and take digestive enzymes to assist with digestion. You can then work with someone who can introduce you to the right supplements to get your gut on track. I found that my compromised gut was due to allergies and bacterial imbalance. I eliminated sugar, processed foods and allergens, and supplemented with some nice herbs to heal the digestive tract and was able to find relief from all symptoms.

Colon Hydrotherapy

I know this is an uncomfortable subject for some, but I've always been very comfortable talking about my poop. My family never told me it was a "no-no" word, and it's just part of life. I also had many gastrointestinal problems growing up. As you may remember from earlier, my family made it part of their business to know how long it had been since my last poop. If they didn't like the answer then I would get an enema. I was not a very good liar, so this happened much more than I'd like to admit. For those of you uncomfortable with the subject, please attempt to hang in there for a couple of paragraphs while I share with you this therapy that has changed my life.

The colon is sometimes referred to as the second brain. One of my colon hydrotherapists calls it the first brain. It's a place where toxins can build up over the years and lead to sickness and disease in the body. Cleansing the colon will not only help gastrointestinal health, but it also positively impacts almost every organ in the body. The liver is a great example. You can actually see the color of the water change to a bright yellow color as the liver is being cleansed. Colon cleansing helps with brain fog, inflammation, and pain as built-up toxins are released.

Colon hydrotherapy—sometimes called colonic—is a therapy that allows warm water to gently pass into the colon to cleanse fecal material from the walls of the intestines. This works somewhat like an enema, but lasts typically around forty-five minutes. As fresh water is going into the colon, you're able to simultaneously release as you desire to rid your body of waste. The first visit can be quite stressful, because the body may show immediate signs of detox, which can include chills, nausea, shaking, and cramping. These will usually come and go during the procedure. After cleaning up the diet and within several treatments, most people find that it's quite relaxing. You feel extremely clean when the treatment is complete. It's almost like taking a shower after you've been working in the yard on a hot day. Think about how good it feels to get all that sweaty mess off the outside of your body. Well, the colon cleanse is the same thing. It cleans years of old toxins and buildup from the *inside* of the body. It's an amazing feeling when the work you do on the inside starts to show on the outside.

WHEN YOU CLEAN UP YOUR INSIDES IT WILL SOON BEGIN TO SHOW ON THE OUTSIDE

I was diagnosed with IBS years before I decided to try colonics, or even knew about it. My doctors were unsure what was causing my pain, nausea, constipation, diarrhea, bloating, indigestion, acid reflux, and skin issues. Why was I taking medications for each of these symptoms if they didn't even know the cause? They never once questioned my diet. They just provided a hand-full of pills to relieve the symptoms (which did not help), and gave me a "catch-all" diagnosis since they couldn't explain the symptoms.

Colonic was something a close family member recommended, and I eventually decided to try it. The initial thought was very scary and I was full of questions about the process. Just like with anything else, you can search for colon hydrotherapy online and watch videos. I did find that once I got on the table, it wasn't as scary as I thought it would be. I'll skip the details of how the process works because you can get that information from your therapist, but I will say that this experience was life-changing for me. After regularly attending sessions, along with cleaning up my diet, I found that most of my negative gastrointestinal symptoms began to dissipate. I was hooked! Not in a negative way, but I knew this had such a positive impact on my health that I refused to give it up.

Now that I've healed my gut, I usually go on a regular basis for maintenance. This is different for everyone and you need to listen to your body for scheduling. Some therapists actually don't recommend a timeline, because they feel your body will tell you what you need. I find that to be true for myself. Once you clean up your diet and heal your gut, and don't need it to relieve symptoms, you may use it to maintain a healthy state. We're constantly exposed to toxins on a daily basis, and this is just one of the ways you can detox regularly. I'm somewhat of a detox junkie. I just love the way I feel when I get all the bad junk out.

Colonic actually detoxes the whole body because the toxins are flushed out of the intestines as well as the kidneys and liver. It hydrates your cells and gives you loads of energy. As we cleanse our bowels of their toxins, we begin to think more clearly, crave less junk, and increase our ability to digest food more effectively. Some use it as a way to jumpstart weight management and help rid the body of disease.

The treatment is very safe, and is not habit-forming. You'll see immediate benefits as well as long-term ones. If you notice your bowels are a little sluggish the next day then that's normal. You can add a little extra fiber to your diet immediately following the session to help prevent that. It may take a little adjustment before your bowels become accustomed to the treatments.

Essential Oils

God has provided us with everything we need on this earth to care for ourselves. He created natural medicines in the form of plants and herbs that surround us. Humans have used the wisdom He has given to concentrate some of these plants into essential oils. There are many companies who produce these oils today and it's important to understand how to choose the best ones. It's crucial to use oils made from plants grown in their natural habitats. This impacts their chemical makeup and healing properties they produce as they're concentrated into oils. When grown in their natural habitat and state, they have antimicrobial properties. Oils made from these plants can be used to treat anything from a headache or cough to cancerous tumors. Yes, I've witnessed many miracles with these natural medicines.

Essential oils have become a part of my everyday life as they have in the lives of many of those I come in contact with on a daily basis. Their gain in popularity has caused cheap imitations to rise in recent years, so be careful and remember that you get what you pay for with oils. I most often use doTERRA oils, but I am also familiar with Young Living. There are other good companies out there, but these are the two I'm most familiar with. I've found that some brands don't perform well at all. Make sure to do your homework before investing in different brands. I've watched others make this very expensive mistake, trying to cut their cost and ended up wasting money on bad oils that didn't produce the same results as their superior cousins. They look pretty pricey up front because of the small size of the bottles, but a little bit goes a long way.

When you purchase therapeutic oils, they can be used for cooking, cleaning, making personal care products, aromatherapy, and are even safe to ingest. Raw honey is great for ingesting oils and it acts as a carrier. You can also put a few drops in a capsule. Rollerballs are great for topical application and can make the oils go a long way. Just mix your essential oils with other liquid oils like coconut, almond, jojoba, or olive oil to act as a carrier. Fractionated coconut is my favorite carrier oil because of how well it absorbs into the skin. Essential oils are fun to learn about, they smell great, and they all have different properties to bring health and healing to our bodies. Essential oils have been used for years and anointing oils were discussed in Exodus 30. The blend described is still used by many today as an anointing oil and in healing ceremonies. There are several companies that have their own blends, and you can always create your own as you learn more about them.

Western medicine has replaced much of the natural therapies like essential oils because we live in a time where we expect immediate response to the therapies we choose. This could mean that we go to a doctor because we have a sniffle and expect him to do something to make it go immediately, or that we go for chemotherapy when diagnosed with something more serious like cancer because that's what we are told works the fastest and is our only option. Most people are too impatient when it comes to natural therapies, because they aren't always immediate. You may have to use a few different oils to see how your own body responds, or may have to apply them every 15 minutes to 1 hour as symptoms creep back in until they are gone completely. It's an inconvenience to some, but it truly is worth the wait and added effort for those of us who want to know we're using the most natural treatment for our bodies instead of poisoning them with medical therapies like prescription chemicals.

Even beyond the biblical use of these oils mentioned in Exodus, we find that oregano and melaleuca were used in the First World War as antibiotics, but they were eventually replaced with pharmaceuticals. Peppermint has been used with great success for tummy upset, which has been replaced with pepto bismol. The more you use essential oils to replace those medications from your local pharmacy, the better your immune system will begin to function. You'll reach a place in your health journey where you'll no longer need cold medicines or anything of that nature because you'll thrive daily in a place of wellness. Building up the immune system is the key to an easy battle when something assaults it. Colds are much easier to avoid than to treat.

Dry Brushing

Dry Brushing is something I've practiced with great results, and is one of the techniques I've used to cleanse the lymphatic system. The lymphatic system is like a garbage dump for the body. It does a great job of sweeping everything up that's toxic. You may have had swollen lymph nodes when you were sick and that's all you know about this system. You should also know that it's necessary to stimulate and detoxify the lymphatic system because it doesn't have a pump to rid the toxins it collects. There are several ways to detoxify the lymphatic system, but a few are skin brushing, massage, rebounding on a trampoline, and vibration plates.

Dry brushing the skin takes about five to ten minutes a day and is easy to add into your routine right before you shower. This is done with a firm, natural bristle brush. They can be found online or at beauty supply stores, and they are fairly cheap. My favorite is the round brush with bristles all the way around the head, instead of the ones with the wooden backs. These tend to have stiff bristles, and you don't have to worry about which direction the brush is pointing. I find I can grip them a little easier and finish the job quicker.

To brush your skin, start at your feet and brush your way up the body in long, circular strokes and move toward the heart. There are some videos on YouTube to help you understand the technique a little better. Skin brushing feels great and makes your skin really soft. It reduces the need for those chemical-filled lotions that ladies love to use to keep the skin from looking dull and dry. It cleans dirt and oil from the pores, and can even be used on the face. Just make sure you have a softer brush or be gentler with the delicate skin of the face. It sloughs off the dead skin, but also increases circulation, which can lead to greater energy levels. It can reduce the appearance of cellulite too. Cellulite is actually from toxins that are in the fat and fascia directly under the skin, so you don't have to be overweight to have it. Brushing helps detoxify the body naturally by stimulating the lymphatic system, which is a part of our immune system.

Soaking

Epsom salts are the main ingredient I use for soaking in a bath. They're very diverse and have been used for years for health and beauty as well as household cleaning and gardening. These salts can be used for pain and inflammation as well as to heal sprains and bruises. The mixture I use for soaking includes one cup of Epsom salt, a little less than half cup baking soda, and about ten drops of essential oils. Lavender, frankincense, and sandalwood are some of my favorite oils to use before bedtime. I also may use cilantro, cypress, eucalyptus, or citrus oils, depending on my goals. Keep in mind that Epsom salts are not the same as table salt, sea salt, or any other type of salt. If soaking in a bathtub is not your thing then you can always opt for a foot bath instead. The key is to get the water as hot as you can stand it and soak for about forty minutes or until the water begins to cool down. This allows time for the toxins to be removed as well as time for your body to absorb the minerals from the salts.

One of the greatest benefits of Epsom salt is that it naturally increases magnesium levels in the body. Magnesium deficiency is very common and contributes to much of the chronic fatigue and heart disease today. Magnesium also has a natural relaxation effect on the body and mind, so it can be really nice after a stressful day when you're ready to wind down for the evening. I love to soak right before bed because it gives me that gentle nudge I sometimes need to rest my mind before going to sleep.

SOAKING IN EPSOM SALT NATURALLY INCREASES MAGNESIUM LEVELS IN THE BODY

Epsom salt also eliminates toxins, including heavy metals. Adding the cilantro oil will assist with heavy metal removal as well. This is a great option if you don't necessarily like the taste of cilantro but want to use it as a detoxifier. Note that you will likely start to sweat while soaking. This is a good thing. I know you probably don't want to think about sweating while taking a bath, but this routine is for much more than cleansing your skin. It's used to detoxify the body. It's important to drink plenty of fluids when doing anything that produces a detoxification effect in the body, so make sure you hydrate well afterward.

I'll close this section with a reminder to not only allow yourself time for a physical soak, but for a spiritual one as well. What I mean by this is just sitting and soaking up the goodness of the God of heaven, or meditate. How do you do it? Just sit and be present with your own thoughts. Open yourself up to hear from God. We live such busy lives, and soaking in the presence of the Lord will renew and cleanse your spirit. He loves when we sit and wait on Him.

You can do this anywhere, but soaking in the bathtub may help you get started because it's a time you've already purposely set aside to relax. It's a great time to put on some relaxing music or some high frequency healing music. Then add some essential oils, and just wait for the Lord. We don't spend enough time in silence, waiting. We live in a world where we feel we must go all the time. This soaking is just a time to replenish your body and your soul. God loves to lavish His peace and love upon us. These are free gifts from Him, so just sit and soak with Him.

Healing Touch and Acupuncture

We not only live in a toxic world, but one filled with many stressors as well. One of the best ways to rid the body of stress and tension is with massage therapy and healing touch. It's also beneficial for decreasing pain, lymph drainage, release of toxins as well as promoting relaxation and sleep. There are many different types of massage, depending on your needs. I personally love the spa-like sessions with hot rocks and essential oils. Some people need additional work and may benefit from deep tissue massages where they work out knots from stress and tension. I used to feel guilt associated with getting a massage because I felt as if I was wasting money and time on myself. I find that it's a great way to force me to settle for an hour to just be present. The benefits of this time of relaxation are endless for the mind and body.

Chiropractics is another healing touch therapy that people tend to love or completely dismiss. I've dabbled in using it throughout my life, especially when I had a lot of inflammation in my younger years because of the consumption of a highly processed diet. Although I didn't realize it at the time, that was the cause of a lot of my pain. I've since eliminated the majority of the inflammatory foods from my diet so I thought chiropractics was a thing of the past for me. That is until I started seeing one as my functional practitioner to assist me with detox and reaching optimal health. On my first several visits to see Dr. Robert Rakowski, we found that my adrenals were working overtime and I was noticing some pretty significant orthostatic hypotension associated with this. That just means the blood pressure drops significantly when going from sitting to standing, and you can feel light-headed and faint at times from the drop. This can be caused by adrenal insufficiency, which for me was the case.

This continued to get worse with every visit, even with everything else moving in the right direction. I was taking the right supplements, doing yoga, meditation, and attempting to live as stress free as possible, but for some reason my adrenals weren't happy and I was physically feeling the effects. Dr. Bob recommended a neck adjustment in attempt to correct the issue. I was thrilled to try anything that might work. This was no ordinary adjustment. He stood behind me on one side while his partner, Dr. Tanae Romportl stood on the other. They simultaneously worked their magic. I will say I thought my neck would never be the same after that (in an almost frightening way), but little did I know how right I was. I have not been the same—but in a very good way. I saw immediate improvement, and over time, I saw 100% improvement. It was a miracle adjustment. I did learn that there is definitely more to chiropractics than what meets the eye. I was amazed that using a technique I thought was just for pain patients could correct a hormonal imbalance in my body. There is great power in human touch.

Acupuncture is another healing practice that's gaining popularity, but is traditionally not used much by those who lean toward Western medicine for treatment. Acupuncture is practiced more in Chinese medicine, and works on the meridians of the body for healing. It can help with a range of ailments. My experience was with shingles. I went through a period of time in my life when my immune system was in the pits. When I was stressed either emotionally or physically, I would get shingles. They appeared on my abdominal area most of the time, but there were a few times when I got them on my face. If you've ever had shingles, you know how painful they are, as well as how long they take to heal. Shingles target the nerve endings, and feel like itchy needles are constantly poking you.

I had a friend who was an acupuncturist who noticed the shingles on my face one day. They had just popped up the day before, so they were very fresh. He asked me if he could treat them with acupuncture. Of course I was willing to try anything. I went to his office immediately, and received my first acupuncture treatment. It was surprisingly not painful at all and didn't take much time. Within a few days, the area was almost completely healed. I couldn't believe it. Shingles is usually present for weeks, and can last months. It typically forms blisters that can ooze pus. Then they scab over and become even itchier. It's a miserable feeling. I know acupuncture can be used to treat many different ailments, but I do swear by it for shingles.

These are just a few examples of my experiences with healing touch therapies. There are many more types out there that I encourage you to explore. Sometimes we live in a box of what we know and if you live in the United States, then that for you is likely Western medicine. That means when we experience anything in our bodies, we turn to a general medicine physician who refers us to a specialist if it's out of their realm, where one of two options typically exist—medications or surgery. Sometimes there's a better option though. I hope my stories here will encourage you to explore your options next time you're faced with an abnormality in your body.

> WE LIVE IN A BOX OF WHAT WE KNOW ... SOMETIMES THERE ARE BETTER OPTIONS TO EXPLORE

The Bible is full of examples where the human touch brought healing. This should be the norm, not the exception. Today, this can happen through a supernatural occurrence, such as prayer and laying hands on the sick as was spoken of in Mark 16:18. Other times, this is through healing touch therapies. Explore this world. God meant for it to be used to benefit you.

Teas and Herbal Therapies

Herbs and teas are something I've discussed a little, but I want you to understand their many benefits. There are thousands of herbs and plants available that have healing benefits. They can be consumed in the form of foods, essential oils, or in teas. All tea is not created equal, just like we discussed with essential oils. Many times the tea bags are the most harmful part because they're full of chemicals. Many teas are also processed with chemicals. I'm not telling you to up your intake of sweet tea made with sugar and Lipton tea bags. I don't really know that it will benefit you at all. I do encourage you to explore some of the health benefits of herbal teas though. It's an enjoyable way to benefit from the healing properties of many of the plants available to us today.

I tend to rotate mine but there are a few I do stick with and use regularly. Holy basil is a wonderful tea that I have used for adrenal insufficiency. Green tea is another one of my favorites. It's a great antioxidant and can help with weight maintenance. It also contains theanine, so it provides clean, balanced energy. Matcha is a more potent antioxidant than green tea, and is wonderful for an afternoon pick me up. You can add it to cold or warm water. It even comes in little packets now so you can add it to a bottled water on the go. My favorite matcha brand is Rishi. They make great loose leaf teas. I use their black teas for making kombucha.

I love the delightful combination I get from mixing my choice of tea with Organo brand coffee in the mornings. I don't tend to use regular coffee because it's pretty acidic and compromises the lining of my gut over time but the Organo coffee is comprised of a little coffee and Ganoderma Luciderm, which is a mushroom known as the "King of Herbs." It's alkalizing for the body, so with that comes countless health benefits, including a natural burst of energy that doesn't leave you with the typical crash that regular coffee brings. It also boosts the immune system, increases metabolisim, improves cardiovascular health, and is a potent antioxidant. I have a link with more information in the references if you want to learn more.

Roasted Dandelion is another great tea. It has a flavor similar to coffee, and helps with liver detoxification. I use it in the mornings as well to perk up my liver. Gynostemma has been used to regulate blood sugar in people with diabetes. Please be careful with all teas, but this one in particular if you are taking medications to regulate blood sugars. Blood sugars should be monitored closely if you're attempting to use this or anything natural as you do not want to drop your levels too low. That said, I am not suggesting you start taking any of these teas or supplements without first consulting your physician.

I use Ancient Medicinals brand tea for its high quality and variety of cleansing blends. Make sure you're purchasing clean tea. Especially some of the tea bags contain toxic chemicals. Loose leaf tea is usually a safer option, but not always necessary or as convenient as the single tea bags. You don't want to waste your time or money drinking toxic tea when the cleaner versions have such great health benefits. Your tea can either be an antioxidant or a toxin, depending on the brand you choose.

I also use Chinese herbal tinctures made from Chinese herbs. Maybe you've heard of some of the popular ones that treat fatigue or other adrenal-related symptoms—like Ashwagandha, Rhodiola, Schizandra. Many times you will find these Chinese herbs in their single form, or in combination with other herbs for specific ailments. I won't go into great detail about these plants, but some of the healthiest men and women who have lived the longest have consumed these plants as a regular part of their diet. You'll find a lot of them used in Ayurveda therapies, which is based on the idea of using nature to bring balance in the body.

A medicinal plant, that grows more dear to me over time is Ganoderma Luciderm. There are hundreds of studies on this mushroom alone, and there is no question as to why the ancients know this as the "mushroom of immortality." I will caution you again to make sure you are buying quality products. I use a brand called Organo. My experience with other brands has shown a definite difference in the results. They use the entire organic mushroom, grown in its native land in the Wuyi Mountains. Their patented shell-breaking technology allows for extraction of 99.9% of the spores from the mushroom, where other companies range anywhere from 2-15%. You can see why their product is naturally more potent.

Why is this mushroom one of my favorites? The testimonies in my own life and the lives of others truly speak for themselves. I've seen relief in symptoms of indigestion, shortness of breath, caffeine intolerance, cold sores, and even protection from sunburn. A study on the effects of protection from UVB rays shows that this personal finding was not by chance.[2] One of the greatest things is when my dentist began to notice that there was virtually no plaque on my teeth during my dental check-ups. Ganoderma is an adaptogen, and can be both energizing and calming— depending on what the body needs. It's alkalizing and decreases inflammation, which you now know are beneficial to almost all disease processes in the body. It also increases nitric oxide, which is important for circulation and energy.

There are countless others who have literally upgraded their life from living with degenerative diseases that are now able to function in daily life. Some I've heard personally that I've also found studies on are symptoms associated with skin conditions like eczema and psoriasis, seizures,[3] diabetes,[4] hypertension, high cholesterol,[5] Fibromyalgia,[6] Alzheimer's.[7] and mental health disorders. I even met a man who said his "once suicidal son" started to consume this product and is now living a full life with no signs of depression or anxiety. It's improving symptoms in children with autism and even multiple sclerosis. The best part to me is its power to enhance the survival and renewal abilities of stem cells.[8]

This means it has the potential for improving every disease process known to man. Honestly, if you want to add one beneficial adaptogen to your life, then this is definitely my highest recommended. There are hundreds of plants that provide us with healing properties just like this one. I tend to rotate the types of herbs I use so I can benefit from a range of God's perfect plants, but Ganoderma is one I stick with for the long-term benefits.

THERE ARE HUNDREDS OF PLANTS THAT PROVIDE US WITH HEALING PROPERTIES

"When a plant's leaves are turning brown you don't paint the leaves green. You look for the cause of the problem ... if only we treated our bodies the same way."

DR. FRANK LIPMAN

C H A P T E R   F I V E

Finding Freedom Through Detox and Moving Your Body

Toxins have a negative impact on us from the way we feel physically to our emotions and cognitive abilities. If you are looking to live in the healthiest state possible, detoxification is necessary. Our bodies are filled with toxins that enter in through the food we eat, the water we drink, and even the air we breathe. We're surrounded by a range of chemicals that are being dropped into our atmosphere as well as EMFs (Electromagnetic Fields) or EMR (Electromagnetic Radiation) from the increase in our use of technology. Even the clothing we put on and the sheets we sleep in are filled with chemicals. Consider our surroundings when indoors—from the paint on the walls to the treatments sprayed on the carpet we walk on, toxic substances are all around us every day.

That new home or new car smell may be exciting, but it's filling our bodies with the very things that lead to disease. Just think, we're wearing cotton which was at one time a plant that was sprayed with pesticides. If not released, this buildup of toxins in the body leads to disease. Toxins are evident in the form of body odor, bad breath, greasy hair, and dull skin. There are many different ways we can detox the body. We'll discuss a few, but this list is definitely not all-encompassing. We cannot avoid toxins completely, but we can decrease our exposure and follow a regular detox protocol that will minimize the harmful effects of those that made their way into our bodies. When we're full of toxins, we feel bad. Sadly, if you've lived with it all your life and never detoxed, you may not even realize just how good you could feel.

Cleanse the Body

One of the easiest ways to incorporate daily cleansing has already been discussed in great detail, and that's by the food we eat. If we eat organic whole foods and minimize the processed junk then that will decrease the amount of pesticides and preservatives we have in our bodies. Drinking water is also important. I prefer reverse osmosis purified water, but it's important to add minerals back in, as the purification process strips the water of its minerals. I also have a unit that structures my water, which turns it into living water as it would appear if it came from a living spring. Dr. Gerald Pollack calls this fourth phase of water "living water," that delivers energy to our cells much like a battery delivers energy.

Our tap water is a dumping ground for pharmaceuticals, fluoride, aluminum, arsenic, and other contaminants that have adverse effects on our health. It's a great start to filter your drinking water, which is fairly common, but also important to filter your shower water. Our skin is our largest organ and is absorbing all the things that are dumped into our public water systems. If you cannot afford to put a filtration system on your whole house, then start with the kitchen sink where you do your cooking as well as your shower head.

When it comes to bottled water, we must consider the Bisphenol-A (BPA) and other chemicals from plastic bottles. BPA has been linked to a number of health concerns, including but not limited to hyperactivity, obesity, altered immune function, and hormone disruption.[1] The "BPA Free" labeling on plastic bottles and drinking cups is very deceiving. What they're not telling you is that it's usually replaced with Bisphenol-S (BPS) or something similar that can be used as a plastic hardener. Some of these are even worse than BPA. These are not limited to plastic water bottles and drinking cups. They're often used to line canned foods and are even used in children's toys. Make sure you're using Pyrex or glass dishes instead of plastic containers to store or heat food. When the chemicals in plastics are heated to high temperatures, they leach into the food or beverage in higher amounts.

There's no way to completely avoid toxins, but there are several supplements that will assist with detoxification. One that I sometimes use is activated charcoal. It has a negative electric charge that causes positively charged ions to bind to it, so they can be carried out of the body. Activated charcoal can come from many sources, so it's important to choose charcoal made from coconut shells or natural sources for healing. Do not use those you barbecue with, which are full of toxins and chemicals. Bentonite clay is similar in the fact that it's a binder that can carry unwanted toxins out of the body. When taking these two supplements, make sure to take them at least one hour before and two hours after other supplements, since they can bind to those as well.

Chlorella is also another great supplement to help with heavy metal detoxification. Our fish are contaminated with heavy metals, so it's always a great idea to add this when you consume fish. Chlorella as well as cilantro help with mercury and heavy metal detoxification. Depending on your needs, you can add others that are beneficial for supporting specific organs or body systems. These are some I use on a regular basis.

It may benefit you to fast throughout the year to exclude things you know you shouldn't eat that may have snuck their way back in. If you're looking to cleanse your body of certain foods, then fasting is a great way. Going cold turkey from all your favorite foods may not be easy, but it will clean out your system and give you a fresh start. You'll notice that cravings for those foods decrease after you remove them for a period of time. I recommend eliminating sugar, grains, corn, gluten, dairy, soy, peanuts, alcohol, and any other foods you know you don't tolerate well. Eggs and shellfish are also highly allergenic, so removing those could prove

DETOX THROUGH FOOD ELIMINATION CAN DECREASE CRAVINGS OVER TIME beneficial. If you've not tested for allergies, it's a great idea to remove all suspect foods to get the greatest benefits.

It's important to give up alcohol because it taxes the liver, and is a major source of weight gain and inflammation. For those of you with a love for soda, it does the same thing. Do you really believe it's okay to drink even now and then? Dr. Daniel Amen says that daily alcohol use and obesity actually decrease the size of the brain—and when it comes to the brain, size matters!

Most of the foods mentioned in the list above also feed certain bacteria and fungi, particularly yeast. Foods that turn to sugar in the body (including alcohol) will feed yeast. Without eliminating them, it's impossible to fully recover from fungal overgrowth in the body. Sugar is a major food source for these bugs, and as long as they're being fed, they will thrive in the body. It's a vicious cycle because the yeast causes you to crave sugar-producing foods, and whether it be carb-filled goodies or sugary treats, the body sees it as the same. The yeast can thrive on either. Once you begin to starve them, they die off and cravings disappear.

I know it seems impossible sometimes, but we are spirit beings, and we have control over the flesh. We just have to tell our body no. We have to stop allowing our mind and its fleshly desires to control us and start taking control of our own thoughts. If we do what we can to improve a little bit daily then we'll eventually make it over the hump.

"For if you live by its dictates, you will die. But if through the power of the Spirit you put to death the deeds of your sinful nature, you will live"

The foods or substances you crave most are usually the ones you need to remove. Get down to a basic diet of meat and vegetables and other whole foods. If you have imbalances in the gut, then you should eliminate or at least limit fruit to only small amounts of berries, lemons, and limes. Small amounts meaning less than one-half cup per day. Studies show that a single exposure to a problematic food can elicit an inflammatory response up to 21 days later. This is why an elimination period of at least 28 days is recommended.

I'll be surprised if you go back to your old eating habits as long as your body is receiving all the nutrients and minerals it needs in the form of food and supplementation. At this point, you can choose to add those suspect foods in slowly to see if there are negative effects. When you fast, truly seek God and He'll show you what you need to remove. Sometimes we also need to consider "non-food" addictions. We are sucked into the world of technology so much that it's refreshing to take a cleansing break from it as well.

To see what the Bible has to say about fasting read Isaiah 58:2-9. If you want more information on fasting, Jentezen Franklin has some great books on the subject. I realized through reading his material that it was not only about detoxing the body, but also the soul. We are spirit beings, and fasting opens up our spirit to receive from God. When we crucify the flesh and give up the things He tells us to, He will help us and we'll be able to move past those addictions and move closer to Him.

Many of the foods mentioned in this section are also acid forming foods. Even too much meat protein can be acid forming. So, when you resume your diet after fasting, try to consume as many plant foods as possible. Cleansing the body by eating a diet rich in green leafy vegetables and other colors of the rainbow will allow you to alkalize the body. When we create an alkaline environment, sickness and disease cannot thrive—not even cancer. Following this guideline of alkalization can be confusing because foods that are acidic outside the body may be alkalizing inside the body.

For example, lemons taste acidic, but help the body become more alkaline. Lemons are also a great way to cleanse the liver. Drinking lemon water immediately after rising is a simple way to wake up the liver first thing in the morning. On the other hand, milk is often mistaken as an alkaline food, but inside the body, it becomes acidic. If you look at natural cures for disease, you'll find a great trend in the promotion of an "all vegetable" diet to jumpstart the healing process. Although I do believe small amounts of meat are good for most everyone, getting rid of those acid forming foods for a cleansing period has proven to be very beneficial.

Mycotoxins

While we're talking about food elimination, I want to briefly mention mycotoxins since they're often missed. A mycotoxin is an organism produced by a fungus commonly known as mold. They can be present all around us without us even realizing it. Mold toxicity can cause symptoms like hallucinations, mood swings, and foggy thinking. I experienced this when I was living in an apartment with mold. I've learned that ingesting mold makes me feel a little drunk. I've experienced it at hotels after drinking out of coffee pots in the room and restaurants. Sometimes it's unavoidable because it's lurking in places we cannot see. Mold causes an allergic reaction for many people though. As with other allergies, we must do our best to remove the culprit to get rid of the symptoms. This may mean getting rid of the foods you're ingesting that are high in mold like peanuts, pistachios, and some coffee. It could also be an office building or damp basement causing the problem. For me, there were many culprits. The goal is to find out what's causing the problem and eliminate it.

THE GOAL IS SIMPLE: FIND OUT WHAT IS CAUSING THE PROBLEM THEN ELIMINATE IT

Mycotoxins can lead to nervous system damage, hormone imbalances, cancer, and other mood imbalances. There are many different kinds of mycotoxins, but there are common ones found in things we may come in contact with on a daily basis. Aflatoxins are often found in peanuts, corn, and cottonseed. Ochratoxins are in grains, coffee, dried fruits, beer and wine, cocoa, nuts, beans and peas. There are also mycotoxin xenoestrogens found in many crops treated with glyphosate. This is one reason bread and grains are a problem for many people. We'll look at xenoestrogens a little later. This is not to scare you away from these foods. It's just to let you know that they may be the very culprits that are keeping you sick.

Break a Sweat

Sweating is another way we can detoxify our bodies. I'm a girl who loves to sweat—at the right time, of course! I just think about all the things I'm getting rid of when I sweat and it becomes much more fun. I believe it's important to do so on a daily basis. As we've discussed, our skin unfortunately allows toxins in, but it can also be a way of escape. I have an infrared sauna in my home that I try to use several times a week. There are immediate noticeable benefits such as increased energy and decreased inflammation. It heats the core body temperature, causing a decrease in toxins at the cellular level. Sitting in a sauna also forces me to relax and take a break. On those days when I have restless energy, or I want more, I take my free weights into the sauna for an extra little workout, which really gets the sweat pouring. I know a sauna may not be an option for you, but the important thing to grasp here is the benefits you gain from breaking a sweat.

When we sweat, we release toxins from the body that cause the skin to look dull. When we rid these excess toxins, not only does it decrease inflammation, but it leads to glowing skin as well. It also improves blood circulation, relieves stress, and helps promote relaxation. Even a fifteen minute high intensity workout will help you break a great sweat if you push yourself hard enough. I believe we all have an extra fifteen minutes in our day. If you don't see where you do, then find something you can cut out to add fifteen minutes, even if it means cutting a little sleep. I guarantee you won't miss it with the added energy you'll receive by replacing it with a workout a few days a week.

I'm so blessed to live in Texas, so it's easy to get outside and pick weeds from my flowerbeds, take a walk, or do yoga in my backyard.

All those things are sure to help me get my sweat session in for the day. Look for ways that you can incorporate it into activities you already do or should be doing.

Mouth Health

There are a few other cleansing techniques that are worth mentioning here that most may not consider. The mouth is very dirty. It's a warm, moist environment, where bacteria love to live. We eat and have leftover food in our mouths and it's a part of the body we need to take care of and clean on a regular basis. There are things we can do daily to maintain good mouth health. Tongue scraping is one of my favorite, and is a regular part of my morning routine. It cleans the bacteria and fungus that lives on the tongue, which boosts the immune system. Scraping cleans the tongue much better than a toothbrush alone ever could. As silly as it sounds, I used to use a washcloth and scrub my tongue a little, so whoever invented the tongue scraper is my hero. This will also help with bad breath, liven up your taste buds, and is great for improving dental health. It's really fun to see all the gunk coming off too.

I try to brush my teeth after every meal. Yes, I'm the girl in the public restroom with her toothbrush. I'm also one of those who carries floss picks and if I can't brush then I at least clean the food out of my teeth. I picked up the habit from my dad, and I must say it's one that I appreciate him passing to me. I cannot stand the feeling of food in my teeth. It's something I'm grateful for because I have a cavity free mouth. Along with brushing your teeth, you can use a waterpik, although I will admit that it's not something I do very often. It works like flossing, but does a better job of getting between the teeth where your floss may not reach. The battery operated ones can be used in the shower, because using a waterpick can be a little messy at the sink.

Oil pulling has gained in popularity and may even be something you've tried a few times and probably just forgot about. It's definitely not something I do all the time, although it's pretty easy to do while taking a shower. The technique is to take sesame, olive, or coconut oil and pull it through the teeth for anywhere from ten to twenty minutes, and spit it out when finished. My favorite oil to use is sesame. It's thick, has a nice flavor, and is said to have the most benefits. I also like it because it's a yellow oil that turns white when you finish—that's because it's filled with all the bad bacteria that were lurking in your mouth that other cleansing techniques could not get to. Please do not swallow this dirty oil when you finish. It's full of bacteria! Spit it out, preferably in a garbage can as the oils could clog your plumbing.

Even though oil pulling is something I admit to doing only "now and then," I do have a great testimony from it. My husband has had his share of dental problems in the past and has had several dental procedures that God knows I could not handle. We were living in Louisiana at the time and he had a dentist appointment on the Thursday before a long weekend. Our dentist did some work on a tooth and decided to wait until a later date to perform a root canal. He was a wonderful dentist and we were all hoping the root canal could be avoided.

Friday, we traveled to Alabama to visit our family for the weekend. He started complaining of tooth pain on the way there. I knew it must be pretty bad because he has a very high pain tolerance, and never complains. We had the dentist call in something for pain, and decided to wait until we were back in town to see him again. My precious husband was miserable, so I pulled out my essential oils and had him apply clove and melaleuca as needed during the day for pain and in attempt to heal his mouth. We also found some olive oil in my dad's pantry and mixed those oils together and he started oil pulling twice a day. By the time we returned on Monday, the exposed nerve was healed. He actually prevented a root canal within a few days. God really has little miracles everywhere. We just have to take advantage of them.

From that time on, I never looked at oil pulling or essential oils in the same way. I knew they worked. I witnessed healing from God's natural plants in such an amazing way. Oil pulling does have other great benefits as well. It not only heals the mouth, but it can reduce heart disease. Bacteria in the mouth can have a negative impact on heart health. If we clean the bacteria that have the potential of traveling to the heart from the mouth, then we can prevent infection in the heart. How many people do you know who have to take prophylactic antibiotics before they have dental procedures? This is to prevent heart damage from the bacteria traveling to the heart. Oil pulling can also reduce inflammation in the body, boost the immune system, and improve acne because of the antibacterial properties in the oils. If it's something you decide to do on a regular basis, it's recommended to do it a few days a week.

I also recommend using fluoride free toothpaste when brushing. Fluoride is one of the most toxic substances in our daily existence and it's been added to our toothpaste as a cavity preventative. You can find it in bottled water, baby formula, and some supplements. Fluoride is also dumped into our drinking water, which is a great reason to make sure the water in your home is filtered. This is a very damaging toxin that's known to cause birth defects, osteoarthritis, cancer, lowered IQ, immune suppression, and is sometimes fatal.[2,3] Studies show that it does not prevent cavities, and is actually known to cause skeletal fluorosis, which leads to brittle teeth and bones.[4] Why in the world are they adding something to our toothpaste and water that causes us to become sick? I have a cavity-free mouth and haven't used fluoride toothpaste in many years.

Environmental Chemicals and Those We are Wearing

There are toxins in our immediate environment that we take in on a daily basis and don't even think about the fact that they're harming us. By the time we get ready to start our day, most people put at least eight products directly on their skin, which are absorbed into the body. Let's consider a typical morning for most individuals. We usually start with unfiltered shower water where we lather soap, shampoo, and conditioner onto our bodies and into our hair. We have our razors that have a conditioning strip as well as shaving cream. Then there's an additional facial cleanser most use, followed by a moisturizer. We follow that by a body moisturizer of some sort and then put on our aluminum-filled anti-perspirant. Makeup is the next step for many of us, and we layer on several different products with that process. We use one or two different products on our hair to create the perfect style. Then we top everything off with a little cologne or perfume before walking out the door. Maureen Rice stated in a recent article that the average woman puts about 515 chemicals on her body every day. This is astounding and quite alarming since many of them are endocrine disruptors, organ irritants, allergenic, and carcinogenic.[5]

Most people don't take into consideration that these products are harming every organ system in the body. It smells so good and makes us look beautiful. So who cares, right? The problem is that our skin is our largest organ, and it's very absorbent. Even the water we're showering in is pouring out chemicals that are being absorbed directly into the skin. Some are so careful to filter drinking water but neglect other sources of water. Then we're wearing ten or sometimes thirty chemicals from just *one* of the many products we slather on our skin every day. Those chemicals are absorbed into the body and have ill effects, leading not only to skin irritations and immediate reactions, but delayed and more serious ones as well. Many of these chemicals have known health hazards like allergies, developmental and reproductive toxicity, and even cause cancer, but are still in most of the products we use today.

HOW CAN PRODUCTS THAT MAKE US LOOK AND SMELL SO GOOD BE HARMFUL?

Sunscreen is another product people use during the summer months or if they're exposed to the sun on a regular basis. Sunscreen actually increases our risk of cancer by filtering out UVB rays and allowing the cancer-causing UVA rays. You may not be getting sunburned by using it, which makes it beneficial, but it's not necessarily protecting you from cancer. I do my best to get out in the sun as much as possible for short periods of time until I know my skin is capable of handling more sun. We should avoid sunburn, but not necessarily the sun. It provides a little healthy-looking glow too. For those with sensitive skin, look for alternatives to those toxic sunscreens.

Household cleaners are another area of concern. Those sold in stores today have the same risks as the products we're using on our bodies. I remember having to use gloves just to clean my house because the cleaners would eat the skin off my hands. They would be red and dry even with the use of gloves. I started making my household cleaners and laundry detergent many years ago, which helped tremendously.

There are plenty of "Do It Yourself" recipes for household cleaners online, and if you want to save money on detergent, that's the way to go. You can make enough detergent to last a year for much less than it would cost you to buy a one month supply of detergent from the store. It's super cheap, and not very time-consuming. If you have more money than you do time, then there are a few brands of detergent you can buy that leave out all the harmful chemicals. If you make your own household cleaners, including an all-purpose cleaner, window cleaner, and furniture polish, adding essential oils is a fun way to enhance your cleaning experience.

Environmental Working Group (EWG) is an organization I learned to love when I was cleaning out some of these toxins and replacing them with more people and environmental friendly products. The website www.ewg.org is a great resource for chemicals in general, but my favorite is their "skin deep" section. It allows you to search products by name and it provides a rating, depending on how toxic it is. You can then click on the rating and see exactly what the toxic ingredient is and what types of adverse effects it causes. They also have a section for food items. You can find an EGW stamp of approval on some personal care products, which is similar to the GMO Project Verified stamp mentioned earlier for non-GMO foods.

Move Your Body

We also have toxins sitting in our bodies because we don't move them enough to keep things moving out. Not just in sweat, but also in our lymph. We don't move our bodies as much or in ways we should on a daily basis. That means getting out of your chair more, even if you exercise regularly. When our muscles are not used, they atrophy and we end up in a place where we would rather sit on the couch all day instead of get out and experience the world around us. It leads to laziness. Simply taking short walk-breaks throughout the day can benefit you greatly. Many of us are stuck behind a desk the majority of the time due to advances in technology. We spend little time on our feet and don't have the very active jobs that our ancestors did. It takes effort to make sure we're moving around during the day.

Experts say that sitting is the new smoking, and that we should take at least 10,000 steps a day to maintain our health. Some offices allow stand-up desks, but we still need to make sure we're moving. Taking a five minute walk break every thirty to ninety minutes is great for the body as well as the mind. We're more productive when we take breaks periodically and do something other than think about work or the task at hand. I know you feel like you don't have time to take a five minute break sometimes, but there are studies that say your mind is refreshed to a point that you become more productive if you take a break than it would be if you continued to work and did not lose that five minutes.[6] From a production perspective as well one of sanity (for some of us), we're better off taking a mental and physical break than continuing to work non-stop.

Movement doesn't stop with a little walking. We need to look for methods to use our body in other ways as well. I like to do squats or some other movement to get blood flowing when I take a break. I remember a physician I worked with would hit the floor periodically throughout the day and do push-ups. It didn't matter where he was. He had a goal and he reached it every day. It worked for him, and he was in great shape and always full of energy. I thought it was a little interesting, but now I think maybe he was on to something. Most of us care way too much about what others think of us and we have a little too much pride to even stand up and stretch our legs during a meeting, much less hit the floor with some sort of exercise in front of our peers. Maybe that wouldn't work in all situations, but restroom break squats are definitely doable, and hardly noticeable. Just find ways to lift your rear end off the chair it's stuck to for most of the day. Your body and mind will reward you in return.

On top of the movements we need throughout the day, we must set aside time a few days each week for more intense exercise. Most people simply don't engage in enough physical activity to maintain good physical health. The best exercise regimen is the one you're going to be consistent with. Your best friend may love weight lifting, but you despise it. If you dread your workout sessions, then chances are you'll skip more than you intend to. If you have a very physical job, then working out may not be necessary. For those who are sedentary most of the day, even getting in an hour workout will not counter all that sitting. That's the reason it's necessary to move more throughout the day as well. It's important to incorporate both. It will also keep your energy up and help with that late afternoon lag that has us reaching for that cup of coffee or the donut holes sitting on the table leftover from our morning meeting.

Do you feel like you don't have the energy or desire to move at all, much less the energy to work out? I understand, because I believe we all have moments like that at times. There was a time in my life when I felt completely exhausted most of the time. I literally started with five minutes of yoga a day until I built up the energy to do more. We all have to begin somewhere. Remember, we have to expend energy to gain energy. The more you add physical activity to your daily life, the more energy you'll gain to do the things you love. If there's not an exercise you love, then find something tolerable and learn to love it—even if you only love it for what it's doing for you. Your chosen attitude will help determine your level of enjoyment.

Try mixing things up a bit. I love high intensity interval training (HIIT) because I can get in a short workout with some weights and high intensity bursts in about fifteen or twenty minutes. I'm pouring sweat by the end, and I know I've really challenged myself. The best part about this type of training is that it has a better overall effect on metabolism and stamina than steady-state cardio exercises. That means it burns more fat over longer periods of time. You'll continue burning fat and building muscle for hours after the workout is complete. Adding resistance or weights is the best way to build lean muscle. Add a little HIIT into the mix and you have a quick, productive workout that no one can make an excuse for missing. I'm sure you can carve out an extra fifteen minutes a few days a week.

Pounding out the treadmill for an hour at a time is very boring to me and I don't see physical changes in my body as a result. The choice between boring routines that produce no results or fifteen minutes of interval training is a no-brainer to me. Doing something that produces results will keep you motivated. People tend to start an exercise fad and stop short of their results because they never really enjoyed it in the beginning, or even attempted to. If you find that you're in a slump and don't exercise as you should, then give it another shot. Maybe you just haven't found the right workout plan.

I also mentioned that I love to do yoga. I practice for about an hour a few days a week. On my busy days, when I know I won't have much time for yoga, I do HIIT because it takes less time. On days when you feel like there's no way you'll get through a workout, just do something anyway. Even if it's light and you can't push as hard as you usually do, it will still give you a sense of accomplishment as well as all the other health benefits in the end. I've never made it to the finish line of my workout and said, "Man I wish I would have never done that." Sometimes I do want to quit though. We're all human, but once I'm in the middle of it and already broke through that first sweat that requires a shower, there is no stopping me. I'm determined to finish. You'll find that same energy when you start seeing results that keep you motivated. Pay attention to your body. If you need a true break then take one. Just don't make a habit of taking too many days off or that will become your new norm.

There are many things we can do throughout the year to spice up our fitness routine. Hiking, bike riding, and kayaking are great summer sports. I'm not much of a winter outdoor person, but some choose to do things in the winter as well like snow skiing. Some of you have children who would love to have you join them in the backyard for a game of catch. There are also social activities that require movement, like local tennis, softball, swimming, or other classes at your local gym. Think outside your normal day to day fitness routine. This will help keep you motivated to move. Even if you decide to skip your intense workout now and then, don't worry. Just stay active.

This is a great time to bring up energy expenditure. I don't suggest counting calories for the rest of your life, but if you're overweight then looking at how much you're consuming compared to how much you're expending is a great idea. We all know about the Fitbit craze, and I'll have to admit, I never really got on board with that for quite some time. I finally downloaded an app on my phone that allowed me to count my steps. This was a great move for me because I didn't realize how little I was moving throughout the day, compared to my thoughts about how much I was moving. We tend to overestimate the amount of movement and underestimate the amount of food we consume. It's just human nature. We want to believe the best about ourselves.

I know there's a lot of confusion surrounding calorie counting and some say we shouldn't bother with it. There's some truth to the fact that if we're eating whole foods and only eating when we're hungry and stopping when we're full then we wouldn't have to worry about weight. The problem is, we don't tend to do that all the time, and since we do underestimate our movement, we may be consuming more energy in the form of food than we are burning off. No matter how you look at it, we need to have a deficit if we want to lose weight. That means we must consume less energy than we burn. This doesn't necessarily mean less calories. It's more about nutrient density. 100 calories of broccoli is not the same as 100 calories of Twinkies. We are not calculators and when we consume whole foods that our body can *use,* over processed foods it *stores,* then we can consume more calories.

There are great apps to assist you in taking a closer look at the types and amount of foods you consume. I like *My Fitness Pal* and *Cronometer* for nutrient tracking and I also use a step counter when I want to get an accurate count of how much I'm moving. I also recommend getting some measuring cups or scales for your kitchen if you're unsure about how much you should be consuming. Remember, we tend to estimate in our favor—even when we're eyeballing our food. I'm not recommending you do this forever, and you may not need it at all, but if you're in a stall losing weight and feel like you're doing everything right in terms of your diet, then you may need to either move more, eat less, or make changes to the types of food you're consuming.

There's a great chance that there's another underlying reason for stalled fat loss, like the need to detox, hormone imbalance, or some other medical condition. Tracking is something you can do without the need for professional assistance though if you're not ready to jump on board with a health professional. There are many people who will tell you that calories don't matter at all, but if you're consuming twice the calories you're burning then it will catch up with you. Mainly because we typically consume unhealthy foods in excess, not the nutrient dense. Maybe it's not the overload of calories that's the problem. It could be that you simply need to move more. Short time tracking can help you get an accurate picture.

Yoga—To Practice or Not to Practice

Yoga has been a part of my life and fitness routine for many years now. I love life much more when I can practice a few days a week. I know you may be wondering how I could possibly talk about yoga as a Christian. So I ask you to get out of your flesh and hear me out. Yes, I've read all the reasons that Christians shouldn't practice yoga. I chose to seek the Father and receive what He had to say and to continue with this practice.

Yoga is a religious practice for many, but it doesn't have to be used in that manner. It's a great way to bring strength and balance into the body, mind, and spirit. Most of our daily activities put our physical bodies in a forward leaning and contracted position. Whether we're bent over at a desk or even working out and running or lifting weights, we hardly ever reach that range of motion that allows the body to stretch in the opposite direction, unless we're mindful about incorporating it. Yoga is a great break from this constant contraction.

WHILE YOGA IS CONTROVERSIAL FOR MANY CHRISTIANS, IT DOES NOT HAVE TO BE A RELIGIOUS PRACTICE— THE PHYSICAL AND SPIRITUAL BENEFITS ARE WORTHY OF PRAYERFUL CONSIDERATION

I've met individuals who needed spinal surgery for instance, and started gently practicing yoga and were able to prevent the surgery. Personally, I've seen in myself a reduction in muscle tension, better digestion, increased strength and flexibility, and not to mention how much more balanced I feel in all areas of my life. I've watched myself develop over time and see improvement every time I practice, which encourages me to keep practicing. This not only occurs in the physical body, but also spiritually. You're able to look inside yourself and ask questions like, "Who am I when I am upside-down? Is there fear, excitement, or a little bit of both when I am faced with a challenge? How can I learn to relax and remain calm through this pleasantly painful burn I'm experiencing?" You realize that you can endure anything for short amounts of time and it strengthens you as a person in all aspects of life when you understand you're capable of much more than you think. It allows you to grow, and growing pains are part of this wonderful journey.

This practice has also taught me about integrity. Many times that's something people lose when under pressure. So often we want to get sloppy when the position we're holding becomes painful. We want to come out of the pose to get relief from that burn. We become tense and it's more difficult to relax during those times of stress on a particular group of muscles. Keeping integrity in this practice also translates into everyday life. We can learn to keep our integrity, even in the face of stress. We learn to be the person we say we are behind closed doors, even when no one is looking. We learn that if we endure the pain, then a greater strength will come. We even learn to relax during those times because our integrity becomes so important to us that we focus there instead of on the storm that is taking place inside us. Yes! Yoga can be a great teacher. This strength also comes from a relationship with the Lord, but I know He speaks to me through my practice. Integrity is just one of those lessons.

I can tell a difference if I ever take a long break from my regular sessions. Yoga decreases stress and certain poses are good for specific ailments in the body. For instance, the shoulder stand squeezes out the blood from the thyroid and allows it to fill with fresh blood when you come out of the pose. This is great for people who have a sluggish thyroid, as I once did. When we put our feet above our heart, it slows the heart rate because it doesn't have to work as hard. This initiates a relaxation response. It's also a great position to find yourself in right before bedtime. Essential oils can be used to enhance your practice. Citrus oils can be used for an energizing practice, or oils like frankincense or lavender can be used for more meditative practices.

Many people have questioned my ability to practice yoga and not allow it to interfere with my relationship with the Lord since it is part of a religious practice. That's a part of the practice I choose not to relate to. We're all spirit, soul, and body. Yoga teaches balance and love and human respect. If Adho Mukha Svanasana (downward facing dog) is a symbol of some form of worship to some then that's their choice. To me it's a place of rest during my intense yoga practice. To me, yoga is a way to move my body in ways I normally would not. It's a time of meditation and relaxation.

I've been released by the Lord to practice yoga. If you're in any way convicted about practicing then that's between you and God. He has a different plan for each of our lives. We're unique individuals and are not all called to the same things. If He tells you not to practice yoga, then don't do it. Just be careful about generally speaking that God does not approve of this practice, or anything else for that matter. It may be that He just doesn't approve for you (for whatever reason), and I'm sure He will even help you understand why if you ask. There are many things that the Father will not allow me to engage in that I watch other Christians do. It's your job to understand what is personal between the Father and you. He's not the same with all His children.

Meditation

We can use meditation to gain access to a full state of relaxation in body and mind. This is a place where we're present, but release ourselves from acting on any passing thoughts or actions. It's a time of reflection. Although you can practice meditation while walking or other forms of movement, it's important to slow your breathing during this time to let your body know it's okay to enter into a relaxed state. Focusing on breath work is also a great way to restore the body and release excess toxins and stress.

When we meditate, there's a change in the pattern of our brain waves. Alpha brain wave patterns promote relaxation, help us to tune in spiritually, and open us up to revelation and truth by bridging the gap between our conscious thinking and subconscious mind. Many of us don't take the time during the day to stop long enough to even eat without answering emails or scrolling through our social media feeds during the meal. I love meditation because it allows me to set aside specific time to stop and be present. It's a great excuse for me to sit quietly or walk and just "be," listening for a moment to what God has to say to me. When we're quiet and listening, we can hear Him so clearly. He's always talking to us.

Be careful with opening your spirit up to just allow anything to come in. There's a difference between active and passive meditation. When we meditate on scripture or open our spirit up to hear from God, focusing on Him or tuning into our surroundings, we are actively meditating. We can also enter into a meditative state while working out or engaging in other activities. This works by becoming present and focusing on the contraction of specific muscle groups. Either way, we are in tune with what is going on in the present moment. Eckhart Tolle has written a great book called *The Power of Now* that will really help you understand how to tap into the power of being present.

Passive meditation is opening your spirit and attempting to free the mind completely of passing thoughts. Men are more apt to passively meditate than women. Passive meditation, and opening yourself up to the spiritual realm with no intention, leaves room for not only good to come in, but also for evil. Philippians 4:8 tells us to meditate on the things that are good and lovely. Doing so restores us.

Meditation is a great stress reliever and can even be done sitting in your car or in a restroom stall at work if you need a 5 minute break from the stress around you. You'll eventually train yourself to escape in the present moment, no matter what's going on around you. That does take a little practice though. Meditation also helps for those afternoon lag times around 3:00 pm when we tend to crave carbs, sugar, or caffeine to get us through the rest of our day. Try walking meditation instead. It will get you over the hump and you won't even miss that latte after a little practice. There are many different types of meditation that can even help with things like a positive mental attitude or weight management as we focus on those things we want to change.

Summing it all up, friends, I'd say you'll do best by filling your minds and meditating on things true, noble, reputable, authentic, compelling, gracious—the best, not the worst; the beautiful, not the ugly; things to praise, not things to curse. Put into practice what you learned from me, what you heard and saw and realized. Do that and God, who makes everything work together, will work you into His most excellent harmonies.

PHILIPPIANS 4:8-9, MSG

CHAPTER SIX

Heedful Living with Ease

We live such fast-paced lives that we forget what it's like to *be* in the present moment. For the most part, we're multitaskers, jumping from one thing to the next to fit everything we feel we need to accomplish into our day. We stretch ourselves so thin that we cannot devote time or energy to one specific thing at a time. This leaves us preoccupied when we should be fully engaged. In turn, our productivity decreases while our stress levels increase. We must find balance to find a peaceful state of rest. God never intended for us to be constantly on the go, running here and there, feeling as if we'll never catch up. His desire is that we enjoy all of our experiences to the fullest, being present and making ourselves available to be used by Him in every situation. To begin to make this a habit, we have to purposely concentrate on being present in all areas of our lives.

Technological Advances

With the advances in technology and the ability to always be connected, it's difficult to stop and enjoy the scenery around us— whether it be children playing, something in nature catching our attention, or even looking at and speaking to the person sitting across from us at the dinner table. God created us to be social beings. Our minds are so used to immediate gratification and immediate answers to everything that we find it difficult to slow down. We have our real life, where we physically engage, but we all have a separate life within social media and the internet. We get caught up in the latest news feeds and are more interested in what's trending than we are what's going on in our immediate surroundings with family or friends. We find it difficult to sit still outside and enjoy the wind blowing through the trees, and birds singing as we feel the warm sun on our face. We don't seem to notice the simple pleasures in life because we've become consumed with technological advances, many times in a very negative way. We have become addicted to constant information, constant entertainment.

There are many reasons these technological advances are having negative effects on our health. Electromagnetic radiation (EMR) is questioned by many as to whether or not it is a real issue, but we're surrounded by it constantly and it's toxic. We even have cell phones and tablets in our bedrooms where we sleep. We surf the internet until it's time to fall asleep and then use our cell phone as an alarm clock, never thinking about the damage these devices are causing. They are lying less than two feet away from us much of the time, even through the night as we sleep.

Then we have our Wi-Fi running all night and day, emitting these signals throughout our homes. Granted, these are low levels of exposure to radiation, but this *chronic* exposure can lead to anxiety, depression, loss of libido, cancer, impaired immunity, Alzheimer's, dementia, heart disease, sleep disorders, and hormone disturbance.[1] Our bodies react to this environmental stress just as they would any other invader, and start attacking. The problem is that we're constantly exposed to this environmental stressor that our bodies never receive a break from. This not only damages the body, but gives it the inability to repair the destruction, leading to disease.

What can you do to prevent this damage? The answer is not very simple since technology is all around us, but turning your devices off in your home is a good start since we spend a great part of our nights there. You can turn off Wi-Fi while sleeping, or at least put your tablet in another room before bed, instead of on your nightstand. Scheduling your phone to flip to airplane mode while you're sleeping will allow you to use your alarm for morning wake-up but not have electromagnetic radiation buzzing around you all night while you sleep. Using microwaves, electric blankets, and heating pads are also harmful habits. Work to minimize your exposure.

Sleep

Technology also interferes with sleep. Our brain waves are active for one hour after shutting down our tablets, cell phones, televisions, or other blue light devices. It's natural for us to receive blue light during the day because it's one of the many spectrums emitted from the sun. The problem is when we continue to expose ourselves to this through artificial light sources during the day and in high amounts after the sun goes down. This typically occurs when we use fluorescent lighting during the day or when we continue to use our devices at night. It interrupts our circadian rhythms. The solution? More natural sunlight during the day, and no technology at least one hour before bed. This means that those of you who are sleeping with your television on are disrupting natural sleep cycles too.

Blue light devices are thought by many optometrists to actually destroy the retinal cells.[2,3] They're already seeing evidence of it in patients today. There are protective eye-glasses as well as screen covers and applications that can be installed on your device to limit the amount of blue light you're exposed to. It's important to use these, especially once the sun goes down to limit your exposure to the blue light.

Use applications that dim the amount of blue light you're exposed to as night draws near, especially if you're on a computer most of the day. You can also use blue light blocking glasses, when under fluorescent lighting for long periods of time. It's been a game-changer for me when it comes to energy, brain fog, and even hunger. Take breaks during the day to allow your eyes time in the natural sunlight when sitting under fluorescent lighting during the day. This is also an excuse to go outside and walk around, so it's good for the eyes and body mechanics. A productive way to multi-task!

Decreasing the amount of light in your bedroom as much as possible when sleeping is essential for maintaining healthy cortisol levels. Even the smallest amount of blue light that may come from a clock or night lights can disrupt cortisol levels and disrupt sleep. When we're not fully rested, it causes daytime sleepiness, which raises the risk for accidents and also leads to symptoms of depression. Sleep is necessary for the body to replenish itself on a daily basis.

QUALITY, RESTFUL SLEEP IS NECESSARY FOR THE BODY TO REPLENISH ITSELF ON A DAILY BASIS

Another thing that interferes with sleep is the lack of a bedtime routine. We understand very clearly that children need time to wind down before bedtime. Most of them are on a bedtime routine, where they may brush their teeth or read a story. This is not a time for them to run around the house screaming and drinking sodas. It conditions them to slow down to rest. When we reach adulthood, we make our own decisions and many times don't realize the positive impact that something as simple as a sleep routine can have.

Dr. Kirk Parsley says it's a good idea to set an alarm one hour before your bedtime and take it as seriously as you do your wake-up alarm. This is to be used as a gentle reminder to you and your body to start shutdown mode for the evening. You can also use this time to prepare for your morning. Pick out clothes, lay out your supplements, and do anything you can to make sure your mornings run as smooth as possible. This allows time to sleep in if you know you're prepared and won't have to rush around doing things last minute. It sure beats feeling as if you can't find anything to wear and forgetting to take your morning supplements because you get up feeling unrested and late the minute the alarm goes off.

Those who sleep less have been shown to consume greater amounts of calories during the day.[4] Sleep deprivation is also linked to many chronic diseases like diabetes, heart disease, cancer, and Alzheimer's disease. Shift work is also considered a carcinogen. That's how important sleep is for the body to recover. If for no other reason, it's a time to start over. I'm sure we've all had those days where we've wanted to crawl back in bed and go to sleep so we could wake up fresh in the morning. Lamentations 3:23 says that God's mercies are new every morning.

Sleep is a time when we pull all the pieces of our lives together and begin to make sense of them by forming long-term memories. Dreams are noted in the Bible on multiple occasions. They also have meaning, which was noted by the interpretation of dreams. It's a time when God likes to share with us, probably because He knows we won't interrupt Him with our own chatter. It's important to experience sleep to its fullest capacity. Stop allowing the enemy to steal your sleep time and your dreams. Learn to appreciate sleep in a new light and it will change how you function on a daily basis. God promises his beloved ones sweet sleep (Psalms 127:2).

Passive and Active Rest

Outside of sleep, we still need to take time to rest. Many of the activities mentioned in this chapter will constitute rest, but this list is not all-encompassing. Rest is what allows us to escape from our stressors. Reading a book is one of my favorite things to do while resting. This allows for a little mental stimulation and also gives me time to do something I enjoy. Sometimes I curl up in my favorite chair with a blanket and a book. For those days when I want a little more active rest, I grab a book, put on my walking shoes, and go for a reading-walk.

I live in a safe neighborhood with plenty of sidewalks, so it's much easier than if you live in a downtown area. It is possible though. You can always find a local walking track if you don't live in a walkable area. This allows you to get in a little more movement during the day as well as some natural Vitamin D from the sun while you gain a little knowledge. This is another great idea for those who love to multi-task. Physical activity increases brain energy, so it's very easy to focus on and absorb what is being read. I know it doesn't sound like rest to some, but it is very peaceful, and if you're reading a good book then you may even forget you're walking. Just be careful and listen for cars! Do this at your own risk and use your best judgement for keeping this activity safe.

Many people use social media as a way to rest. Be careful what activities you choose to do during your resting time. I know social media is fun sometimes, but we all know how easy it is to get sucked into scrolling a news feed. We look up and an hour has passed. I've found that I could be a lot more productive with my day if I take breaks from social media. I encourage you to temporarily restrict yourself from it to see just how many times a day you want to look at it. I think it's a bigger time-waster than most realize. There's a lot of garbage that gets posted to those sites. The things we choose to read and listen to are very powerful in shaping our future. Those things get buried into our soul and literally become a part of who we are. Be careful little eyes what you see!

Mindful Eating

Do you eat when you're not hungry? Do you overeat or crave certain foods when you're going through an emotional down or upswing? Too bad we usually don't crave broccoli. Our cravings are for the sweet, salty or carb-filled foods. Gluttony or addiction to food is real. If you answer yes to any of the questions above, then learn to investigate your hunger or cravings. Many times we just eat because we need to fill a void. If it's true hunger, then give the body nutrients. If you're not sure, then drink a glass of water. Many times we are just dehydrated and the body signals hunger to let us know. Maybe your constant hunger is a spiritual void. Most people eat bad foods at the wrong times because they're lacking something else. It's not necessarily the food they desire. We must find the root to take control of the cravings and addictive behaviors.

LEARN TO INVESTIGATE YOUR HUNGER OR CRAVINGS— FIND THE ROOT CAUSE OF THEM

I love the work of Eating Psychologist, Marc David. He has a great understanding of how healing it is for the body when a person lives in a constant state of presence. He focuses on the psychology of food and teaches others how to eat with intention. Loving oneself is in the center of the work he does. This includes stopping and setting aside the rest of the world when we eat. It means no working lunches or watching television during dinner. He believes that we should rest and digest during a meal instead of eat mindlessly while we multitask. As you probably fully understand by now, I'm a lover of good time management and even multi-tasking, when it's productive. Eating is not one of those times for me. I don't like to be rushed during a meal and if that's the case then many times I'd rather not eat at all. My husband likes to say that I need time to properly masticate my food. It's true!

Digestion begins in the mouth. We should chew our food until it's no longer possible to detect what it was. It should mix with our saliva so that the body's digestive enzymes go down with each swallow. If we properly chew our food then it will make the digestive process easier on the body. It's hard work on the body to break down food that we've scarfed down and swallowed whole. It leads to gas and bloating and other forms of nasty gastrointestinal distress. If you're so hungry when you eat that you have a hard time slowing down, then consider the reason. Are you eating something your body is addicted to and it's like a drug, like sugar? Are you really that hungry because you've waited too long to eat, or is it possible you are overly hungry because you've been eating the wrong foods and you don't have good control over blood sugars? If so, even when eating the right foods, you won't obtain the proper balance of blood sugars or appropriate nutrients to send satiety signals. Once you correct the issue, slowing down becomes enjoyable.

Many people have started replacing meals with shakes and smoothies. It's one of my favorite ways to get in more vegetables and added nutrients, but many times they're filled with too much sugary fruit. We also need to think about our digestion when we consume these delicious beverages. Sometimes we think of them as a quick meal, but no matter how convenient they may be, we must remember to chew them as well. They still require the mixing of saliva to properly prepare the body for digestion. The mouth is where the first release of digestive enzymes begins, which are needed to break down our food into forms the body can use.

Eating slowly allows you to quickly realize when you're full. It takes time for the gut signals to reach the brain to say, "Okay, I've had enough," and if you're scarfing your food then you'll likely finish your meal before the body has even had time to react. If you learn to slow down, you could eat half the meal instead of the entire thing and experience the same feelings of satiety, without being overstuffed. Think about what you're eating. Taste each bite fully. Learn to appreciate the true flavors of the food and spices as they mix together. I know I mentioned that we seek too much pleasure from food, but keep in mind we were discussing the garbage like fake sugars and such, as well as food addictions. It's not that I believe food should not be enjoyed. It's important to learn to enjoy and appreciate "real" food though.

No matter what your mind tells you, you don't have to eat the entire pan of fresh baked chocolate chip cookies or polish off that bag of Cheetos! I know how it is. Please trust me on this. Remember, I am the one who used to buy a BIG chocolate chip cookie and finish the whole thing in one day. You have the ability to put it down. Once you start to think about what you're putting in your body and what your body is actually using it for, then you'll be able to make better choices. You can still mindfully eat your sweet treats too though. You'll also find that you're more satisfied with less when you do. It's your mind and many times your imbalanced gut bacteria that's telling you "I want more and I want it as quick as I can get it." Just start saying, "I do not desire to eat more than my body needs to survive. I refuse to overeat!" Take control over your body and mind. As much I believe we have to have the right mindset though, much of this is related to an imbalance in the body. I encourage you to work with someone who can help you clean up your gut too. There are very powerful studies on the fact that we cannot depend on human will-power alone to get us past these moments.[5] We still must find the root to our consistent poor choices and work on that before we resolve the problem.

Stop Stress and Worry

Are you living with chronic fatigue? Are you a constant worrier? Does your mind race around your to-do list, preventing you from falling asleep? I'm almost certain you can say that either you or someone you know has been affected by stress on a personal level. I know for me, I was taught to worry. It's been passed down in my family from one generation to the next. It's something I've had to work very hard to overcome.

Do you know that peace of mind is a free gift? It's true! John 14:27 tells us that it's a gift the world cannot give and tells us to not be troubled or afraid. Worry is a tactic of the great deceiver to rub salt in our already wounded hearts when we have something that's not going as we think it should. It's something we've all experienced at one time, and is very real. It can cause physical symptoms in the form of rapid heart rate, nausea, diarrhea, or anxiety as an immediate response to a very high stress situation. We can also have chronic stressors in our lives that cause more serious conditions like stomach ulcers, heart attack, stroke, skin irritations, and psychological disturbances.

Constant stress leads to poor adrenal function and may bring on other symptoms like feeling overwhelmed, craving salty foods, low blood pressure, feeling dizzy upon standing, mental fog, decreased sex drive, slowed healing, low blood sugar, depression, PMS symptoms, poor concentration, and feelings of indecision. Shall I go on? There's a gamut of symptoms that can be caused from stress. Taking the time for rest and relaxation is crucial when these storms come along. We must learn how to take authority over them and our mind as we're dealing with life stressors. I like to think, "What is the worst thing that could happen to me right now?" when I'm experiencing a stressful situation. I usually find that the worst possible outcome is not really as bad as my mind would have me to believe initially.

We also have to remember that God knew us before we were even born.[6] He knit our very being in our mother's womb.[7] He knows our end and our beginning.[8] He knew every hardship we would face before we even took our first breath. He also cares about those things that are important to us. He wants us to live a victorious life.[9] He will not let us fail if we trust in Him and let Him guide the way.[10]

With all that being said, why should we stress? If He is going to take care of the ravens, then are we not much more important than they are?[11] If you give good gifts to your children, does He not have the ability and desire to give even greater to you?[12]

> *"Do not worry about anything; instead, pray about everything. Tell God what you need, and thank Him for all He has done. Then you will experience God's peace, which exceeds anything we can understand. His peace will guard your hearts and minds as you live in Christ Jesus"*
>
> PHILIPPIANS 4:6-7 NLT

Stop stressing! You may say, "Well that's easy for you to say. You do not know my situation." Whether I know your situation or not, I do know that guilt and worry come from the enemy. Allowing stress and worry to have a place in your life is a way of saying, "God, I don't trust you!" So many people's lives are literally destroyed because of stress and worry. I've had to painfully watch it happen even in my own family. If I could shake it out of them I surely would. I've been there myself—under that generational curse of stress.

It's a lie from the enemy. He wants you to feel that the whole world is about to crumble under you. It makes you unproductive. It's an easy portal into your body to bring in not only worry, but sickness, when you open yourself up to his lies. Depression comes because you see your situation as hopeless. Ahhh ... but that is a lie from the enemy as well, because God tells us plainly, *"For I know the plans I have for you. They are plans for good and not for disaster, to give you a future and a hope."*[13] He tells us we have a future and a hope! So let go of the stress and enjoy all the goodness God has in store for you, today.

Relationships

God created us as relational beings. He not only wants a relationship with us, but He desires for us to have relationships with others. He calls us his family for a reason. Believers are known as the bride of Christ. Some of us can be called children of God. He says in Genesis 1:28 to increase and multiply in the earth, whether that be with biological or spiritual children. We are not made to "do life" alone. You're not capable of doing everything on your own, and you never will be, no matter how hard you try. It's not how you were created. We need each other. Many times we want to do things on our own because we have this irrational belief that no one can do it as well as we can. Perfectionism and being a control freak leads to stress, which we know has serious physical consequences. Learn to let go of that control and share it with those around you.

Think about your life and the enjoyment you receive from listening to the stories of those around you. It's also true that you have something to offer others. You never know what that cashier is going through or if anyone has genuinely cared about whether or not she's having a good day. She may not have anyone to empty her heart out to. I've noticed that if I'm willing to listen, then people are usually willing to talk. It's amazing what others will share with you. It's a great time to learn, reflect on another life that God created, and to appreciate the life and story of another. People are sometimes hesitant to open up to others because it's rare to find someone who genuinely cares about what's going on in their life. We all know how hard it is to open up to others sometimes, so when someone chooses to do that with you then listen to them and respect their willingness to do that.

Just as technology compromises sleep, it can also be a factor in the quality of our relationships. We're often so caught up in our devices when we're in public that we don't engage with the world around us. We have our own little inner circle and those outside it don't seem to deserve our time. We're too busy to stop and enjoy the other beings that God created. We judge them by the way they look, and even by what they say. We need to get out of our flesh and start appreciating people more for who they are. I'll tell you that I was as great a sinner as I am a saint. I have tattoos and had piercings and the scars to prove my days of rebellion. I'm not ashamed of who I was and if today I want to dye my hair the color of the rainbow and color my skin with ink then that's what I'll do. It doesn't change my heart. Be careful little mouth what you speak… about others before you even have a chance to know them.

I remember thinking that I didn't have anything to offer others. I'm not sure where this feeling came from, but I remember feeling "different." I remember being told I was different and some people even used the word "weird" to describe me. I looked at it in a negative way instead of realizing that God created me to be unique. When you believe that no one understands you because you're "uniquely different" then you're listening to a lie from the enemy. You were created by a God who loves you more than you could ever imagine. He has great plans for you. You are His favorite child! He has commissioned you to do great things on this earth while you're here. He sent you for this special time. Do not allow the enemy to steal the destiny that God implanted in you.

"Have regular hours for work and play; make each day both useful and pleasant, and prove that you understand the worth of time by employing it well."

LOUISA MAY ALCOTT

CHAPTER SEVEN

Self and Spiritual Awareness

We are spiritual beings. God created us in His image, and He is a spirit-being. We were meant to enjoy life as such. It's said that humans only use a small percentage of their brain. I believe that's because much of the brain is made to engage with the spirit realm, and we don't train ourselves to use it. We're conditioned to believe that this world we live in is all there is and is what really matters ... this is far from the truth. The body will pass away, but the spirit will live on forever.

Spiritual Root of Disease

Spiritual awareness is one of the most overlooked areas when it comes to healing the body. Many times it's not only the body that needs healing, but also the soul. There is a spiritual root to all disease. It's so easy now with access to the internet to search for the spiritual root of illness. Are you suffering in your body? It's likely that you are if you're reading this book. Maybe the same malady has plagued you for years. Maybe it's something that has plagued your family for generations. Physical manifestations in our bodies reveal to us what's going on spiritually. If we only focus on the physical then we may never get to the root. Healing is about reaching a place of wholeness—in spirit, soul, and body. It's something that happens over our entire lifetime and the more wisdom and insight we receive, the more whole we can become.

As I was writing this book and nearing the end of the journey, my career put my writing on hold. I lost my job because of my decision to not vaccinate. This consequence added a lot of financial and emotional stress. I stopped writing during this time because I didn't have the desire or energy to do so. I was in a depressed state—feeling like the victim. Yes! I went there. The Lord then blessed me with a contract job where I worked about eighty hours a week. The state of financial stress lifted, but there was no time to write. I was so close to finishing this assignment from the Lord. How could I possibly put this on hold again?

At the end of the two month period, I found myself in a very rough place physically. I was one of the healthiest people I knew —eating right, sleeping great, exercising daily, keeping my positive attitude, thinking right—so I thought. I was doing everything I knew to live the healthiest life I knew how. The problem? I let myself slip into that state that I used to live in nonstop: perfectionism. I was putting so much pressure on myself with my subconscious thoughts about where I should be with my writings and how I was letting people down and letting God down. Many of my friends contacted me during this time and asked me when the book was going to be published and I felt like a failure telling them that my writing was on hold ... again!

I noticed symptoms of fungal overgrowth creeping back into my body. How could this be happening? I pray for the sick and see them recover. Why was this happening to me and why could I not make it stop? When I finally took the time to sit down with my loving Father-God to ask for His wisdom, He took me to the spiritual root of my issue. Even though most of this was in my subconscious, it was still impacting me physically. It wasn't what I was eating or that I was not resting appropriately. It was simply the manifestation of the repressed anger that I was not even aware of. I was angry with the fact that I didn't have the time to write, yet I chose to accept the contract and work those long hours. It was my victim mentality and the unconscious belief that I wasn't good enough. It was the strive for perfectionism and outside approval that I thought had left me so long ago. It had crept back in and the symptoms were literally attacking me with a vengeance.

Next steps? Well, this is where life takes us all on a different journey and yours will almost always be different from mine. My physical body did need a cleansing in the natural, but it also needed spiritual cleansing. I pray over my physical body every day. I speak *affirmations*. I take communion. But there are times when we need to focus our attention on specific areas so we can gain understanding and knowledge from the Lord as to why we're stuck at a particular crossroad. The outcome of this particular lesson for me has a lot to do with nurturing the self and obtaining emotional healing to gain physical healing. Just like God, we are three in one—spirit, soul, and body. It takes nurturing all three to obtain wholeness.

I tell you this story to remind you that you have brilliant gifts that God has given you to use on a daily basis. You are never behind, even if you feel there's a delay in reaching your goals. In my own story, He knew I wouldn't accomplish this task on the timeline I set for myself. Your setbacks are no surprise to Him, even if they are to you. God is always on time, so we have nothing to worry about. Worry opens the door for the enemy to enter in and when that happens, we're asking for trouble. It's important to enjoy life—break out in song and dance sometimes. Maybe even do it in the rain. Do something that will pleasantly shock those near you. It's life's little pleasantries that bring us such joy. Those of us who are serious, deep thinkers tend to forget that sometimes.

YOUR SETBACKS ARE NEVER A SURPRISE TO GOD, EVEN IF THEY ARE A SURPRISE TO YOU

So why am I telling you all this? The bottom line is that there's a spiritual root to all illness. Our sins, sickness, and disease have been paid for already, but the door to the demonic can be opened knowingly or unknowingly. It can be opened by something personal or even by our ancestors, which can come upon us in the form of a generational curse. I like Dr. Dale Sides' explanation in his book, *Exercising Spiritual Authority*. He uses the acronym TRUCOPS to explain the ways spirits or strongholds can enter into us. I hope you'll check out the book in its entirety, but for now, the acronym stands for Trauma, Rejection, Unforgiveness, Curses, Occult practices, Physical objects, and Sin. When we come to the understanding of what gave that demonic force the legal right to be there, we can exercise our spiritual authority to remove it.

Appreciation for Nature

One of my favorite things to do is yoga in my backyard. I dreamed of having a home with a beautiful yard. I asked the Lord for a palm tree and he gave me eight! I have a privacy fence and when I get ready to escape, it's me, my patio, yoga mat, palm trees, tropical plants, and the beautiful blue sky. It's my own personal getaway when I'm home. I can go there and escape into a place of total peace. When we were looking at homes, I walked into this backyard and knew it was the place for me.

I never had a true appreciation for nature until my husband and I went on a trip to Guatemala. We went hiking to the top of the San Pedro Volcano on Lake Atitlan. It was a wonderful experience. We had a guide who had a love for nature like I had never witnessed. I watched him spot things I would have never noticed as I was huffing my way up this mountain in a brand new altitude for my lungs. The longer we hiked, the more I enjoyed his passion for God's creation. He spotted flowers and pointed out his favorite trees. He spoke about the critters we could hear and about the ones who lived in the area.

About half-way up the mountain I began to realize it was a choice to have this appreciation. I began to notice the different types of plants as I touched the trees and felt the different textures. I started to enjoy the change in the weather as we approached the top. I looked at the other mountains from a distance and noticed the beauty in what I could see close up versus what those same mountains looked like from a distance. I listened to the creatures singing to us as we walked through the place they called home. It was a beautiful experience that changed my life. I'll never see God's creation the same. He made it for us to enjoy, so make sure you experience it to the fullest.

There's something special about being outside, touching the plants and the living things that God made. It actually gives us energy and life. In the world we live in today that's filling the body with toxins and free radicals, we need to have this time to reground our bodies. What is a free radical? Free radicals form when an electron is unpaired, so it will try to steal from another molecule in an attempt to stabilize itself. We don't want to completely eliminate them, but producing fewer of them in the body is the goal. There's a great deal of scientific information on free radicals if you care to research it, but I'll keep it simple for now.

Free radicals can form in the body when we're exposed to things from the environment like poor diet, stress, alcohol, or exposure to air pollutants. The most common type is oxygen free radicals. They're responsible for damage to the cell membrane, which can lead to premature aging, cancer, and cell death. These are secreted into the body anytime there's an assault that would lead to inflammation. This even includes simple things like running into something and getting a bruise or injury. Free radicals are what cause the inflammatory response, where we see pain, redness, swelling, or heat in an area. These free radicals are actually leaking into the tissue and causing damage, causing the inflammation.

There is a technique called "grounding" or "earthing" which allows you to transfer free electrons from the earth to the body. It has amazing antioxidant capabilities. Shoes—even the minimalist ones—will block this conduction because of the rubber or plastic soles, and we wear them constantly. The grounding technique is very simple. Remove your shoes and walk barefoot on the ground. That's it! The benefits of touching the earth with your feet are endless. It can actually prevent the need for the inflammatory response to even take place in the body and allow healing to occur naturally. It's also good for anti-aging, and helps the blood to clot appropriately, which helps balance blood pressure. It's beneficial for heart disease as well as brain disorders such as dementia for the same reasons—all related to blood clotting. The best place to practice grounding is at the beach or near water, or in grassy areas. Exercising or gardening barefoot outdoors is a productive way to accomplish this.

Frequencies

I'll briefly mention something that's been one of the most interesting things I've studied. It has the ability to tie in most of what we've already discussed. Our body runs off frequencies, which are measured in megahertz (MHz). What we subject ourselves to throughout our day has the ability to increase or decrease those frequencies. Disease can live easily in lower frequencies, and heaven operates on higher frequencies—a great explanation as to why there's no disease in heaven. Certain disease states thrive when the frequencies in the body are at particular levels. It creates an atmosphere they want to exist in.

There are many different ways to increase frequencies in the body. With a little research, you'll find that musical notes have different frequencies. There are certain musicians who play music within a specific range to bring the body into a state of calmness or relaxation. Others frequencies provide healing or energy. For example, 528 MHz is said to bring healing and DNA repair. We also find that processed foods have low frequencies, while whole foods have higher frequencies. Canned food and dry herbs have a frequency of zero. Regular coffee has a negative effect and actually lowers your frequency by about 15 MHz within three seconds of drinking it. I can definitely tell a difference in the way I feel now that I am drinking a healthier coffee. My rule now is pretty simple—healthy coffee or no coffee. Negative thoughts can decrease measured frequencies by 10 MHz, while positive thoughts increases by about 12 MHz. Prayer and meditation increases measured energy frequencies by about 15 MHz. Some of the highest frequencies are found in essential oils. Australian blue cypress has a frequency of 530 MHz. Rose oil comes in at 320 MHz, and Frankincense at 147 MHz.

You can use essential oils to raise the frequencies in foods. For example, if you choose to have a cup of organic coffee, then you can add drop of therapeutic grade cinnamon essential oil. Cinnamon is great for balancing blood sugar and has a lovely taste. I take a liquid multi-vitamin/mineral, so I sometimes add a drop of frankincense to that, especially since I've learned about frequencies. Just to give you a reference point, a healthy body should have a frequency of

62-68 MHz. The flu has the ability to invade the body at 57 MHz, cancer at 42 MHz, and death occurs at about 20 MHz.

The higher we keep our frequencies, the better. The awesome thing is that this ties together everything else we've already discussed. We can have high frequencies in the body by eating clean plant foods, using essential oils, playing relaxing and healing music, and doing all the other healing activities we have discussed. I love to use high frequency music when meditating. It really helps me enter into that meditative state quite easily. We can create an environment where disease cannot thrive. I encourage you to look into this more. This knowledge had me so excited I was dancing around my back yard when I got the revelation.

Power of Words and Thoughts

"You always attract into your life the people, ideas, and resources in harmony with your dominant thoughts."

-- BRIAN TRACY

We are what we meditate on and speak out. If we say and believe we are fat, tired, sick, broke, and unsuccessful, then we become those things. In other words, we can become our greatest fears when that is what we meditate on. I prefer to say that I am the righteousness of God[2]. I am the head and not the tail, above and not beneath.[3] Everything I touch prospers.[4] His word tells me to decree a thing and it will be established.[5] So I decree that I am beautiful and that I have the heart of God. I am fulfilling the destiny He has called me to. I am a loving wife and a cherished friend. I am prosperous in all my ways. He wants the best for me and His plans for me are good. They are to give me a hope and a future.[6]

If those things are difficult for you to say then start with something easier. "I do not have to eat the entire box of chocolate chip cookies. I can lose that extra weight. I have the desire to balance my hormones, start an exercise regimen, eat healthier, be a better spouse and friend." You are who you believe you are.

"The tongue can bring death or life; those who love to talk will reap the consequences."

PROVERBS 18:21 NLT

YOUR WORDS ARE SO POWERFUL THEY EVEN IMPACT THE LIVES OF OTHERS

Your words are so powerful they even impact the lives of others, whether you realize it or not. God created with His words. *"In the beginning, God created the heavens and the earth."*[7] ... *"Then God said, 'Let there be light, and there was light.'"*[8] The Bible tells us that we are to be imitators of Him.[9] He created us to create. He created words to create. So we are to use our words to create. I could write an entire book on this subject, so I won't go into any more detail here, but if you would like more information on the subject, then I highly recommend Charles Capps book called *"Tongue: A Creative Force."* I want you to understand that your words and thought patterns do matter.

When we talk negatively about ourselves or others, those words stick to the very soul of a person. Even if you're speaking behind someone's back, those words still matter. Speak life into those you love. I know it's easy to get caught up in gossip with others, but it feels so much better to know you have a clean heart and haven't been part of opening the door for the enemy to bring defeat in another person's life.

We've all been guilty. For instance, your friend is on another diet. She talks about it every time she sees you, and you really don't care to hear it anymore. She's excited one minute about losing weight. The next minute, she's shoveling in the Oreo cookies. You say, "Oh here she goes again. It's the same as usual. She'll fall off the wagon soon enough and gain her weight back." I cringe when I hear people who don't understand the power of their words speak defeat over another's life. Your words do create. Stop it! Speak out that you believe things will be different this time. Break the power of all the negative words you've spoken into their lives before. If you can't do that then stop talking about the situation period. Gossip brings destruction.

I've witnessed miracles where this is concerned when word curses have been broken off of people. I'll tell you about a man I know. His whole life, people spoke that he was not good enough. He would never amount to anything. He was lazy. He could never hold a job. He would need someone to support him forever. Those were lies from the enemy. This man was very capable of contributing to society. He was just in a place where he was taken care financially and never expected to do anything with his life. He did have the desire but didn't know how. He was forced to look for a job when he lost his parents and couldn't find employment that could even offer him a decent roof over his head with food on the table. The Lord spoke to me about him and showed me that word curses were what had been holding him from success. When we broke those curses and spoke new words of life into him, his life changed. He called me shortly after with news about his great full-time job and how much his life had improved. No more depression either! Praise God! Our words truly create. They can bring life or they can bring death. You choose.

Visualization

Visualization is used by many of the most successful people. There's real power in being able to see yourself in the place of success you desire to be in, before it ever happens. This can apply to many aspects of our lives from seeing ourselves healed and whole as well as in a state of financial freedom. This can also be applied to spiritual and emotional aspects of life as well as any other area. If you see yourself sick and living in poverty, then there's no surprise as to why you may be living in that state. If you see yourself as a success in your career and in health, then the likelihood of you obtaining that goal is much greater.

We can tell ourselves day to day that we're depressed, and when those feelings come we have a choice to meditate on those thoughts or meditate on who God says we are. We can look at ourselves as a sad mess or we, as believers, can straighten our crown and remember who our Daddy is! We can choose to believe what the enemy and the world and the current state of our body are telling us or we can choose to believe what God's unfailing word says. We do have a choice, and making that choice puts great power behind its fruits. I'm not saying we should ignore the reality of what's taking place in our lives, but we should be able to look at the other side of our current negative state and work to obtain it.

Being able to see myself the way God sees me has been beyond powerful in my life. It opened the ability for me to distinctly see who He destined me to be. Now I am walking that out little by little on a daily basis. As I complete a small piece of the puzzle, He gives me another. Now I'm able to see the fun in the journey. You can do the same.

Once we make the choice to believe what God says about us, the next step is easy. We just need to see ourselves in that role. That's the visualization piece. God gives us desires because He wants us to reach for those goals. If you have a particular goal in mind and are looking to reach it, then seeing yourself in that position is a first step to accomplishing it. This could be in the form of a vision board or some other physical object you look at daily. This could also be in the form of creating pictures in your mind and seeing yourself in this new position, or dressing the part as you're on your way to obtaining it. I do all of these things, but for me, this is also getting up every morning and calling myself who God says I am: healed, righteous, prosperous, kingdom minded, physically strong, bold and courageous. I am a lover, friend, confidant, teacher, promoter, and creator. Every morning, I choose to look at myself in the mirror and visualize myself as these things and more as I speak these truths. This is power!

If you create a vision board then you must look at it and meditate on it. You can't just create it and stuff it in a closet or a room you never go in. I've created a rotating vision board. It's a large piece of cork board with pictures of my dreams. They're pinned up and when I reach that goal, I remove the picture and replace it with another. I have a file of my old pictures so I'm reminded of the power behind this activity. I travel a lot, so I have a picture of the board with me and I look at it and meditate on it regularly. I speak out those things on the board as if they're true today with "I am" statements. My board has the word "believe" on it as well as a picture of a crown and a heart that always stay in place. When I finish making my "I am" statements, I follow it up with, "I believe the King has placed these things in my heart." I know these visions are not my own and He has placed them inside of me. When we begin to seek Him with our heart, our desires will line up with His.

> A VISION BOARD HELPS YOU VISUALIZE YOURSELF REALIZING YOUR GOALS

The brain has cells called mirror neurons that respond in the same way when we perform a particular action as they do when we witness someone else perform a similar action.[1] Vision boards can also create this same benefit when you look at the pictures and visualize yourself completing the goal. This vision stimulates the mirror neurons in areas that control consciousness and motivation. When looking at your vision board, speaking out *afformations* is also beneficial. This concept was developed by Noah St. John. He says that if we turn our affirmations into a question—or *afformation* —then it leads us to search for an answer on how to obtain it. So if instead of looking at our vision and saying, "My home is filled with beautiful treasures," we may ask, "Why is my home filled with beautiful treasures?" This forces us to come up with an answer, even if it's only in our subconscious. It's given me a refreshing look at the visions for my future. We have to remember that just because we create a board with visions, doesn't mean there's some magical force behind them making them happen. We still have to take steps to make them a reality. This idea of *afformations* makes us think about how we will accomplish them.

Spending Time with Our Creator

We did talk about relationships with others, but we also have a Heavenly Father who is always waiting for us to meet with Him. He's there to guide us in every decision we need to make, if we seek Him. A major part of my healing journey came to fruition when I truly started seeking Him for answers. He draws us to Himself. In the beginning, I didn't even realize it was Holy Spirit leading me on this path to wellness. Oh, but when I did … what a joyous day it was for me! Then I knew I could ask and He would give me all I needed to become well. He's always ready to listen and respond to us, so that means we must listen to Him as well. Did you know our viral load actually drops when we have a relationship with God? The work of Dr. Caroline Leaf is absolutely astounding, so if that last statement interests you at all, I encourage you to look at some of her work.

Maybe you don't fully understand what it means to *know* God. Maybe you just know *about* Him. Maybe you wonder why I found the need to reference scripture so much as I shared my own healing journey with you. I understand. I was there at one time too. All that can change today though. You can come to know Him as the God who loves you, heals you, teaches you, and guides you on your own journey the way He has me on mine. If you want to know Him today and have never asked Him to be a part of your life, I want to give you that opportunity. After all, that's the most important part of our journey. So I invite you to be part of our heavenly family. I invite you into the kingdom, to be one of God's children.

Pray this with me today: "Heavenly Father, I know You are my creator. I know You have great plans for me. I believe You sent your son to die on the cross for my sins, sickness, and disease. I know this all happened so I could have an abundant life. Your word tells me in Romans 10:9 that if I confess Jesus as Lord and believe that He died for me and that You raised him from the dead then I will be saved. So today, Father, I believe and I receive this free gift from you. Come into my heart and save me. Come into my life and lead me. I am Yours. Guide me from this day forward in all You have for me. Amen!"

If this is the first time you've said this prayer, then congratulations on making the best decision you could have ever made during your life on this earth. Welcome to the family of God. Go tell someone who will help you take the next steps and find a church home you can grow in. Read the Bible and seek Him with all your heart and He will fulfill all your desires.[10]

Joan Hunter has a book called *Life* that I know will bless you and teach you how to begin your walk with Him.

CHAPTER EIGHT

Really, What is the Secret?

The secret is simple. *"Trust in the Lord with all your heart, lean not on your own understanding. In all your ways acknowledge Him, and He will make your paths straight"*[1] The most important thing I do is not worry about what others think about my lifestyle choices. I allow Him to direct me, and He keeps me on the right path. What does it really cost to live a healthier lifestyle? From the food I eat to the way I move my body—those choices are mine. Many times we shun what is different because maybe we're afraid of or don't understand it.

I used to take offense every time someone questioned me for living differently. I didn't want people to notice I was different. Now I embrace and seize it as an opportunity to teach. I know how my lifestyle changes have made me new, and I realize now that God brought me through it to share with others. Many hard lessons of following the rules that were set by others led to many painful years of sickness and disease for me. I'm now a walking testimony to God's faithfulness if we listen to and obey His word. I will not turn away now that He has brought me through. I owe Him more than that.

I feel better than I ever remember feeling in my entire life. I haven't been vaccinated in many years. I also cannot tell you the last time I had even the slightest hint of a cold. If I ever get itchy ears, a tickle in my throat, or the sneezes, those symptoms may last at most a few hours. By that time, my immune system has taken care of whatever caused it. I get plenty of sleep, drink no less than 120 ounces of water per day, include plenty of healthy fats, vegetables, protein, and micronutrient rich foods in my diet. I limit my sugar intake, exercise no less than five days a week, move as much as possible, appreciate nature, meditate, and love the Lord with all my heart. I don't stress over pleasing everyone around me anymore and I focus on what I want for my own life. If you don't take care of you, then no one will and you won't be around to help care for others. It really is okay (and actually preferred) that you put your mask on first—as the flight attendants remind us each time we fly.

IF YOU DON'T TAKE CARE OF YOU, NO ONE ELSE WILL

Preparation is key. Prepare your heart and make a decision that you want to make this lifestyle change and take small steps to do it. Once you've embraced small step one, start including small step two. Prepare your mind. You may question your decision when the going gets tough. You will likely have a desire to give up and just eat that cake. You may even be tempted to quit. If you have prepared your mind ahead of time and accept the fact that you will face challenges, then when they come, you'll be able to push through. Even if you mess up, it doesn't mean you're completely defeated.

Keep pushing toward your goal. Prepare your food. When you go to the grocery store, buy vegetables and immediately prepare them before putting them in your refrigerator. Prepare hummus or guacamole or whatever it is you like to dip raw vegetables in. When hunger hits, you're more likely to make a healthy choice if you can grab that as quickly as you can your unhealthy snack. Prepare for your day. Getting your food ready for the next day is easier when it's a part of your evening wind down routine. Pack leftovers for lunch when cleaning the kitchen at night. If that's not a good time for you, then pick a time that is. Take your lunch with you and you won't be tempted to stop quickly at the closest fast food place to grab lunch between meetings. Benjamin Franklin said it well. "If you fail to plan, you plan to fail."

Communion

I take communion on a regular basis. Some like to call this the meal that heals. I believe that's true. I have a special place in my home where all my study material sits, and my communion cups are within arm's reach at the place where I spiritually dine with Jesus. If I don't have cups with me and I feel the need to take it then I simply visualize the act and I know that God works through that as well. Communion actually changes our DNA so that we become more like Jesus. It heals our physical bodies, but also brings about change in our characteristics so we become more Christ-like. I do this to remind my body that no sickness or disease has a right to live inside of me because that was already paid for when Jesus died on the cross. It's a reminder that Christ lives in me, so I can carry Him into the world— everywhere I go.

When I take communion, I speak in faith, praising the Father for what the elements are doing as they enter my body. The bread brings healing. Anywhere in my body that I need physical healing, I visualize it patching up the gut, conditioning the adrenals, decreasing inflammation, eradicating bad cells or infection, and purging toxins from the lymphatic system. There may be different needs the Father brings to mind and I just speak those things out as He impresses on me to do so, knowing and believing that everything I'm speaking is taking place in the body. Then I take the cup and see the blood of Jesus running through my veins— changing me and molding me so that my characteristics line up with His. I intentionally become more like Jesus every day. The blood that forgave me allows me to freely forgive others so I'm not plagued with the bondage that comes along with unforgiveness.

These are just a few of the things that I do when I take communion. There's no exact science or perfect way. As you mature in your relationship with Him, it will change the way you do many things. He teaches us and we are to respond to that new knowledge. Some days you may feel the need to repent during communion. This repentance is not a bad thing. It's what draws us closer to Him.

The way you take communion can look very different and still be in line with what He wants for you. We are to listen closely to see how He leads us, especially during this intimate time with Him.

Healing Hands

There's great power in the laying on of hands. I've witnessed many miracles in my own life as well as the lives around me just by following what scripture says about the healing touch of God. The Bible tells us that we will lay hands on the sick and see them recover.[2] It's amazing to see people walk in using a cane and leave leaping for joy because the Lord healed them in their back and legs. I've seen legs grow out and spinal columns straighten, all with simple words spoken with authority, in Jesus' name. I've experienced emotional and physical healing in my own life.

I previously walked in fear and intimidation and lived with depression, hopelessness, anxiety, and a lack of self-esteem. I'm free from all those things today because my good and gracious Father God took those things from me, just because I asked Him to. Much of the healing came by way of prayer and healing touch from others who believed God's Word when it said they would see the sick recover by the laying on of hands. Do you think prayer is nothing more than emotional support for an individual or something we just do? Well, think again. One study found that healing prayer was able to dissociate the memory of the feelings associated with trauma, as evidenced by changes in the precuneus region of the brain.[3] This is one of many other studies that shows physical evidence of the power of prayer.

I've seen change in other areas simply by laying it at the feet of Jesus, knowing He cares for me and has already paid the price for all the enemy has plotted against me. It's nice to hear others comment on my confidence levels, because I'm reminded of how far I've come with God's help. I've also experienced immediate freedom from symptoms like shortness of breath, pain, unforgiveness, and a broken heart. I had kidney stones twice and had surgical procedures both times to break up stones because they were too large to pass. The third time, I refused to go through that stress again. I simply took dominion over those symptoms and spoke healing into my own body and the symptoms left, never to return. I still felt God nudging me to do a few things in the natural. Within a few days of receiving that word and acting in obedience with a few supplements He recommended, I *painlessly* passed a very large kidney stone. I was healed! He has also shown me natural ways to cleanse the kidneys so I can keep them healthy moving forward. The healing power of God is real, and it's still alive today and available for you. Believe it's for you and you'll receive it too.

Unforgiveness

Unforgiveness is many times a root of sickness and much of the emotional pain we live with daily. Disease is the result of a spiritual root. Once we find the root, we can rid the disease. I've seen people have pain in their spine with no evidence of a medical reason for their pain according to MRI, and when they walk through a forgiveness exercise the pain goes away. There are many ways stress, pain, and sickness can come upon us. If you're finding it difficult to receive and keep your healing, then I suggest you search your heart. The Father is willing to forgive us, and He wants us to experience the freedom that comes along with forgiving those who have hurt us. Remember, you're the one suffering from the unforgiveness you're harboring, not the person you're unwilling to forgive. So free yourself from that today by speaking out loud your forgiveness toward them, and feel the weight of that burden be lifted from you.

Jesus freely forgave us, and He expects us to do the same.[4] Offering forgiveness doesn't mean that we agree with the person who wronged us, or that we even believe they're sorry for what they did. Forgiveness means that we intentionally let go of the offense and any emotions that are tied to it. We don't wish harm on them or that they will receive negative payment for their actions, and we wish them well. We simply let God handle it instead of holding on to it and attempting to handle it in our own minds or with our own actions. The words may come easy, but you may have difficulty asking the Father to bless the one you oppose. This

FORGIVENESS OPENS THE DOOR TO WALKING IN DIVINE HEALTH

is important though, because when we release them to the Father and ask Him to bless them, then we are truly able to let go of all the pain associated with the negative memories. We remember that we are not so perfect ourselves.

Sometimes we have to forgive the same person multiple times because there's so much pain or anger. I've walked through the same forgiveness prayer many times for some of the same people who have hurt me. There's such freedom in letting it go though. I'm happy to say today that I'd gladly sit and dine with anyone who has hurt me in the past, because Jesus literally took all the pain away. What relief that brings!

What's really beautiful is when the Lord shows you the other side of the story. Maybe He reveals the reason for the other person's pain. It could have nothing to do with you, but it could stem from something very painful in their own lives. This insight is an open door for you to pray for and bless those who curse you.[5] The healing of these types of wounds often leads to repentance as well. Maybe we're not always as innocent as we would like to think we are. When we search ourselves, the Lord will reveal our hearts and will correct us in a loving way. He leads us to a state of repentance to draw us closer to Him. His kindness is meant to lead us to repentance.[6] We are to purify our hearts,[7] and cease to do evil.[8]

We must come to God with clean hearts. Repentance is often looked at in a negative way—as if we have to apologize to God for doing something wrong. That's not the reason behind repentance at all. This belief is actually a form of pride, and pride is the downfall of man. If we're carrying old sins and unforgiveness from the past, our hearts are not pure before Him. His desire is to take us deeper into Him. This becomes easier when we seek Him on more than a surface level. Then when the pride attempts to creep in, we'll see it for the ugly spirit it is.

Jesus Loves You

I cannot stress enough the importance of a relationship with the Lord. The rest of this information pales in comparison. He'll give you the desires of your heart as they line up with His when you seek Him with all your heart. He lavishly loves you and He desires you more than you could ever imagine. He's waiting for you to come to Him like a little child and spend time playing in His presence. When we release our praises to Him and we begin to worship Him for who He is, then we'll see a shift in our circumstances. Things will begin to change in us and around us. We become so focused on His beauty that we forget our current circumstances, or at least we realize that in the great scheme of things they don't matter as much as they once did. He becomes our everything. He rides on our praises. Thank Him for what you do have and watch Him shower you with more of His unfailing love as your heart becomes more gracious for all He has done for you.

"Seek first His kingdom, and all these things shall be added unto you."

MATTHEW 6:33

Jesus died not only for our sins, but He also bore our sickness and disease on that cross over two-thousand years ago. It belongs to you. When you received your salvation, did you pay anything for it? No! Your healing is the same. You make choices every day that allow you to live in health or not. I would rather have health any day, but healing is also available, and it still works today. What's even better is that you can also become whole in body, soul, and spirit. It's all available to you.

It's up to You

You are responsible for the things you know. So now that you have this information, it's up to you to do something with it. Maybe you feel like dumping all the junk out of your cabinets and starting over. If that's not realistic for you, then decide what is and start there. We all have very different needs, but do something today to start. This is a lifestyle change. This is not another fad diet or trend. This is the truth about what God has placed here for you to stay in health.

One of the things I know is that Holy Spirit will guide us if we listen. Once you receive your healing, ask if you can make changes in your own lifestyle to keep it. He'll lead you. I can promise that the things in this book are a good start. Satan will attempt to steal this word from you if he can. He has destroyed our food as a way to enter into our bodies and destroy them. If you've been healed of diabetes and you choose to put chocolate cake in your mouth with every meal then the likelihood of your glucose remaining under control is not great. It's a very simple concept. I'm not saying that God can't heal us over and over—because His grace is sufficient—but He also teaches us how to stay well and resist the attacks of the enemy. If Satan can find a portal, he will enter. God didn't promise us an easy road with no temptation but he did promise He would provide a way out when we were tempted ... even with sugar! Even Jesus was tempted. He just resisted. Submit yourself to God, resist the devil, and he will flee.[9] You cannot keep doing the same things and expect different results. God will heal you, but you must do your part.

Today, I choose to take authority over my body and tell it what I need it to do. I put the right things in to nourish it and am always asking Holy Spirit if I've done something to open myself up to negative symptoms if I get them. I'm great at listening to my body in regards to what it needs, but that knowledge comes from

Him. I constantly speak harmony and balance over my body and its chemicals, electrical and magnetic frequencies, as well as the hormones. I speak to my pH levels, oxygenation levels, or anything else that I need to on a daily basis. Tell your body what you need from it, believe that it will listen, and watch for the miracles. Remember Jesus is our healer!

I'll leave you with this to think about. When someone asks about our health, why do we feel the need to explain why we are sick, rather than say why we are healed? Remember the power of your words and those things you meditate on. When we explain our sickness, we're justifying the enemy over what God has already done for us. You are in charge of your health and healing, not the enemy. Stop handing it over to him.

I've experienced healing in such a way that I'll never be the same. I know God put everything I need to thrive on this earth and I'm opening myself up to learn more about it as He further reveals His truths to me. This book does not include everything I've learned, nor do I know everything He has in store for us to be whole. I do hope it gives you the start you need to begin to experience healing in your own life though.

I pray that you're empowered to make the changes necessary to live in divine health, the way God intended you to. I pray this knowledge will seep out of these pages into you and you'll soak up this information like a sponge and have the strength to apply it to your daily life. May you see yourself the way God sees you - completely whole—as He teaches you about all aspects of healing the whole man, which encompasses the spiritual, physical, social, emotional, mental, intellectual, and environmental parts of your being. May you know the purpose for which you were called and have a greater understanding that what the enemy has meant for harm was never God's plan for you. He is love and He is ready to lavish it upon you if you will let Him. He is a gentle God and will not force himself though. So welcome Him with loving arms and receive all He has for you. It is His delight to bless you!

"I know it is God's will for me to live in divine health. God's Word brings life to my body and health to my flesh—therefore I abide in it. Sickness and disease do not come from God and they are not part of His plan for my life. God's plan for me is abundant life!"

KENNETH COPELAND

RESOURCES

Chapter 2: Today's Medicine

- Ty Bollinger - Author of *The Truth About Cancer* book as well as Docuseries

  https://TheTruthAboutCancer.com/

- Suzy Cohen - America's Most Trusted Pharmacist Author of *Drug Muggers; Thyroid Healthy; Diabetes Without Drugs,* and others

  https://SuzyCohen.com

Chapter 3: Food and Nutrition

- Vani Hari - Health Food Advocate/Investigator

  www.FoodBabe.com

- Environmental Working Group - Exposing toxic substances

  www.EWG.org

- Non-GMO Project - Non-GMO Food Verification

  www.NonGmoProject.org

- Cornucopia Institute - Researchers in sustainable and organic agriculture

  www.Cornicopia.org

- Eating Well Guide - Directory of local restaurants, farms, and sustainable food

  https://www.EatWellGuide.org/

- Cherie Calbom - The Juice Lady, Author of *The Juice Lady's Guide to Fasting; Souping is the New Juicing;* and others

  www.JuiceLadyCherie.com

- Suja - Cold-Pressed Organic Juice

  https://www.SujaJuice.com/

- Dr. Terry Wahls - Functional Medicine Doctor - Healing chronic autoimmune disorders

  https://TerryWahls.com/

- Mountain Rose Herbs - bulk organic herbs, spices, and essential oils

  www.MountainRoseHerbs.com

- Jeffrey Smith - Comprehensive GMO Health information source Director of Genetic Roulette - The Gamble of our Lives

  www.ResponsibleTechnology.org

- Contact your senator - voice your concerns

  www.Senate.gov/senators/contact

- Petitions for change

  www.Change.org

- Dr. Josh Axe - *Food is Medicine* - Natural remedies, healthy food, fitness, supplementation

  https://DrAxe.com

- Dr. Joseph Mercola - Take control of your health - accurate, up-to-date health source

  www.Mercola.com

- Cronometer - Nutrient Tracker - allows for vitamin and mineral tracking

  https://Cronometer.com

- Dr. Peter Osborne - Gluten Free Society Author of *No Grain, No Pain*

  www.DrPeterosborne.com

- Dr. Mark Hyman - Director at Cleveland Clinic's Center for Functional Medicine, Author of *Eat Fat, Get Thin; Blood Sugar Solution; 10 Day Detox Diet*

  www.DrHyman.com

- Dave Asprey - Biohacker. Creator of Bulletproof Diet, Author of *The Better Baby Book; Bulletproof Diet; Head Strong*

  www.Bulletproof.com

- Dr. David Perlmutter - Empowering Neurologist, Author of *Grain Brain*

  www.DrPerlmutter.com

- John Douillard - Natural Health News and Ayurveda, Author of *Eat Wheat*

  www.LifeSpa.com

- Dr. Tom O'Brian - Certified Gluten Practitioner, Author of *Autoimmune Fix*

  www.TheDr.com

- Local Harvest - Online Farmers Market

  www.LocalHarvest.org

- Eat Wild - Online meat and vegetable Farmers Market

  www.EatWild.com

- US Wellness Meats - Online organic meat market

  www.GrassLandBeef.com

- Marine Stewardship Council - Certified Sustainable Seafood

  www.MSC.org

- Tom Mueller - How to buy great olive oil

  www.TheTruthInOliveOil.com

- Thrive Market - online discount health food store

  http://Thrv.me/Chelsie

- Jordin Rubin - *The Makers Diet*

  www.JordanRubinHealth.com

- Theresa Shields Parker - Christian weight loss coach, Author of *Sweet Grace, How I Lost 250 Pounds*

  www.TeresaShieldsParker.com

- JJ Virgin - Exposing Hidden Sugars

  www.JJVirgin.com

- Gary Taubes - Author of *The Case Against Sugar*

  www.GaryTaubes.com

Chapter 4: Alternative Therapies

- Drucker labs - complete liquid nutrition - Multi-vitamin/mineral

  www.Store.DruckerLabs.com

- Living Fuel - Protein and nutritional meal replacements

  www.LivingFuel.com

- Xymogen Pharmaceutical grade supplements

  www.Xymogen.com

- Metagenics pharmaceutical grade supplements

  https://Metagenics.com/

- Numedica pharmaceutical grade supplements

  www.Numedica.com

- Thorne Research Supplements

  www.Thorne.com

- Healthforce Nutrients - Greens, Protein, Algae

  www.HealthForce.com

- Organo - Coffee, tea, supplements, shakes - featuring Ganoderma Luciderm (Reishi) superfood

www.Chee1231.MyOrganoGold.com

- Doterra

https://MyDoTERRA.com/ChelsieWard

- Young Living Essential Oils

www.YoungLiving.com

- Ancient Medicinals Herbal Teas

www.AncientMedicinals.com

- Rishi Teas

www.Rishi.com

- Dr. Robert Rakowski - Chiropractor, Kinesiologist, Certified Clinical Nutritionist, Certified Biological Terrain Instructor, International lifestyle and natural medicine lecturer

www.TheDrBob.com

- Sayer Ji -Green Med Info - Science of alternative medicine

www.GreenMedInfo.com

- Dr. Eric Zielinski - *Regain Your Health God's Way*

www.DrEricZ.com

- Dr. Anna Cabeca - OBGYN, Regenerative, Anti-Aging Medicine Expert, Mighty Maca Superfood Greens

www.DrAnnaCabeca.com

- Dr. Sara Gottfried - Women's Health Functional Medicine Doctor, Author of *The Hormone Cure; The Hormone Reset Diet;* and *Younger*

www.SaraGottfriedMD.com

- Dr. Tami Meraglia - Functional Medicine Doctor - How to balance hormones naturally, Author of *The Hormone Secret*

www.DrTami.com

- Dr. Izabella Wentz - Overcome Autoimmunity Naturally, Author of *Root Cause* and *Hashimoto's Protocol The Thyroid Secret* - Documentary
  www.ThyroidPharmacist.com

- Dr. Alan Christianson - Integrative and Adrenal Health, Author of *The Adrenal Reset Diet*
  www.DrChristianson.com

- Yuri Elkaim - Making Fit and Healthy Simple Again, Author of *All Day Energy Diet* and *All Day Fat-Burning Diet*
  www.YuriElkaim.com

- Niki Gratrix - The Abundant Energy Expert, Expert on Adverse Childhood Trauma Scoring
  www.NikiGratrix.com

- John Immel - Ayurveda Medicine
  www.JoyfulBelly.com

- Solutions for Sustainable Living and Gardening
  https://eartheasy.com/

Chapter 5: Finding Freedom Through Detox and Moving Your Body

- Dr. Gerald Pollack - Author of *The Fourth Phase of Water: Beyond Solid, Liquid, and Vapor,* Founder and editor-in-chief of the scientific journal, Water

- Dr. Daniel Amen - Brain health - Psychiatrist, Author of *Change Your Brain Change Your Life; Brain Warrior's Way;* and others
  http://DanielAmenMD.com

- Christa Orrechio - Candida and gut cleanse, Author of *How to Conceive Naturally*

  https://TheWholeJourney.com

- Doug Kaufmann - Know the Cause - Mold and Fungus, Author of *The Fungus Link; Eating your Way to Good Health*; and others

  www.KnowTheCause.com

- Jentezen Franklin - Fasting, Author of *The Fasting Edge; The Spirit of Python; Fear Fighters;* and others

  www.JentezenFranklin.org

- Jason Fung - fasting - "The Complete Guide to Fasting"

  https://idmprogram.com/

- Eckhart Tolle - Mindfulness, Author of *The Power of Now*

  www.EckhartTolle.com

- Wellness Mama - Simple "Do It Yourself" home remedies

  https://WellnessMama.com

- KNOW Vaccines - Kids Need Options With Vaccines

  www.Know-Vaccines.org

- National Vaccine Information Center - Unbiased truth about vaccines

  http://www.NVIC.org

- *Vaxxed - From Cover Up to Catastrophe* - Movie

  http://www.VaxxedTheMovie.com

- Dr. Meryl Nass - Physician - Sharing truth to empower

  http://AnthraxVaccine.Blogspot.com

- Gaia - Online Yoga Studio

  https://www.Gaia.com

- BodyRock - HIIT personal training from your living room

  www.BodyRock.tv

- Tim Ferris - Author of *The 4-Hour Body; Tools of Titans;* and others

  https://Tim.blog/

- Ben Greenfield - Personal Trainer and Coach, Author of *Beyond Training* and others

  https://BenGreenfieldFitness.com

- Clearlight - Infrared Sauna

  https://InfraredSauna.com

Chapter 6: Heedful Living with Ease

- Marc David - Psychology of Eating, Author of *Slow Down Diet; Nourishing Wisdom* and others

  http://PsychologyOfEating.com

- Trudy Scott - Certified Nutritionist - overcoming eating anxiety, Author of *The Anit-Anxiety Food Solution*

  www.AntiAnxietyFoodSolution.com

- John Assaraf - Neurogym - helping others reach their potential with God-given abilities, Author of *Having it All; Neurowisdom* and others

  http://JohnAssaraf.com

- Dr. Kirk Parsley - Sleep

  http://www.DocParsley.com

- F.LUX - Blue light blocker for computer

  www.JustGetFlux.com

- Dr. Caroline Leaf - Cognitive Neuroscientist - Mind-Brain Researcher, Author of *Switch on Your Brain* and others

  http://DrLeaf.com

- Joan Hunter - Healing Evangelist, Author of *Healing Starts Now; Life; Freedom Beyond Comprehension* and others

  http://JoanHunter.org

Chapter 7: Self/Spiritual Awareness

- Dr. Dale Sides - Liberating Ministries for Christ International, Author of *Exercising Spiritual Authority* and others
  http://www.LMCI.org

- Barbie Breathitt - Breath of the Spirit Ministries, Author of *Dream and Symbol Interpretation* and others
  https://www.MyOnar.com

- Charles Capps - Author of *Tongue: A Creative Force*
  https://www.CappsMinistries.com

- Patricia King - Author of *Decree* and others
  http://www.XPMinistries.com/Patricia-King/

- Noah St. John - Boost performance through positive afformations, Author of *The Book of Afformations* and others
  http://NoahStJohn.com

- Cal Pierce - Director of International Association of Healing Rooms, Author of *Receive Your Healing and Reclaim Your Health* and others
  http://HealingRooms.com

- John Tussey - Wholetones - High Frequency Healing music
  www. JohnTussey.com

THE GREATEST GIFT YOU CAN
GIVE YOUR FAMILY AND THE
WORLD IS A HEALTHY YOU.

—JOYCE MEYER

ENDNOTES

Chapter 1: How it All Began

1. https://wire.ama-assn.org/education/whats-stake-nutrition-education-during-med-school

Chapter 2: Today's Medicine—Where Have We Gone Wrong?

1. https://www.cdc.gov/flu/about/qa/vaccineeffect.htm
2. Seek the Kingdom of God above all else, and live righteously, and he will give you everything you need (Matthew 6:33).
3. https://www.ncbi.nlm.nih.gov/pmc/articles/PMC2768420/
4. http://www.ncbi.nlm.nih.gov/pubmed/10547175
5. http://www.ncbi.nlm.nih.gov/pubmed/26184290
6. https://www.ncbi.nlm.nih.gov/pmc/articles/PMC2908269/

Chapter 3: Food and Nutrition

1. http://www.accessdata.fda.gov/scripts/cdrh/cfdocs/cfcfr/cfrsearch.cfm?fr=101.22
2. http://www.ncbi.nlm.nih.gov/pubmed/23090335
3. http://www.i-sis.org.uk/MicePreferNonGM.php
4. https://www.ncbi.nlm.nih.gov/pubmed/22337346
5. http://www.dailymail.co.uk/health/article-1388888/GM-food-toxins-blood-93-unborn-babies.html
6. https://www.ncbi.nlm.nih.gov/pubmed/16357623

7. https://www.ncbi.nlm.nih.gov/pubmed/26725064

8. Sci Transl Med. 2010 Jul 21;2(41):41ra5

9. https://www.ncbi.nlm.nih.gov/pmc/articles/PMC3479986/

10. http://detoxproject.org/glyphosate/glyphosate-is-everywhere/

11. https://www.ncbi.nlm.nih.gov/pubmed/3356636

12. https://www.ncbi.nlm.nih.gov/pubmed/1400008

13. https://www.ncbi.nlm.nih.gov/pubmed/22150425

14. https://www.ncbi.nlm.nih.gov/pubmed/14710168

15. http://www.ncbi.nlm.nih.gov/pubmed/20676364

16. https://www.ncbi.nlm.nih.gov/pmc/articles/PMC1931610/

Chapter 4: Alternative Therapies—Healing Practices Forgotten by Western Medicine

1. https://ods.od.nih.gov/factsheets/Magnesium-HealthProfessional/

2. https://www.ncbi.nlm.nih.gov/pmc/articles/PMC5355704/

3. https://www.ncbi.nlm.nih.gov/pmc/articles/PMC4092074/

4. https://www.ncbi.nlm.nih.gov/pmc/articles/PMC5437617/

5. https://www.ncbi.nlm.nih.gov/pmc/articles/PMC4980683/

6. https://www.ncbi.nlm.nih.gov/pmc/articles/PMC2768420/

7. https://www.ncbi.nlm.nih.gov/pmc/articles/PMC5233449/

8. https://www.ncbi.nlm.nih.gov/pubmed/21055951

Chapter 5: Finding Freedom Through Detox and Moving Your Body

1. https://www.ncbi.nlm.nih.gov/pmc/articles/PMC3220783/

2. http://poisonfluoride.com/pfpc/html/symptoms.html

3. http://www.slweb.org/bibliography.html

4. https://www.ncbi.nlm.nih.gov/pmc/articles/PMC3956646/

5. http://www.dailymail.co.uk/femail/beauty/article-1229275/
    Revealed-515-chemicals-women-bodies-day.html

6. University of Illinois at Urbana-Champaign. "Brief diversions vastly
    improve focus, researchers find." ScienceDaily. ScienceDaily, 8 February
    2011. <www.sciencedaily.com/releases/2011/02/110208131529.htm>.

Chapter 6: Heedful Living with Ease

1. http://www.who.int/peh-emf/about/WhatisEMF/en/index1.html
2. https://www.ncbi.nlm.nih.gov/pmc/articles/PMC2831109
3. http://www.tsbvi.edu/instructional-resources/62-family-engagement/3654-effects-of-blue-light
4. http://www.huffingtonpost.com/2012/03/14/sleeping-calories-eat-study_n_1345232.html
5. https://www.psychologytoday.com/blog/real-healing/201608/food-addiction-is-not-about-willpower
6. https://www.ncbi.nlm.nih.gov/pmc/articles/PMC3510904/

Chapter 7: Self and Spiritual Awareness

1. https://www.ncbi.nlm.nih.gov/pmc/articles/PMC3510904/.
2. 2 Corinthians 5:21.
3. Deuteronomy 28:13.
4. Deuteronomy 30:9.
5. Job 22:28.
6. Jeremiah 29:11.
7. Genesis 1:1.
8. Genesis 1:3.
9. Ephesians 5:1.
10. Psalm 37:4.

Chapter 8: Really, What is the Secret

1. Proverbs 3:5-6.
2. Mark 16:18.
3. https://www.ncbi.nlm.nih.gov/pubmed27515886.
4. Colossians 3:13.
5. Luke 6:28.
6. Romans 2:4.
7. James 4:8.
8. Isaiah 1:16.
9. James 4:7.

M E E T   T H E   A U T H O R

Chelsie Ward has a background in applied behavior analysis. Her study of the psychology of the mind has helped her devise  successful behavioral intervention techniques to help others succeed in reaching their health and wellness goals. Her career as a nurse (BSN, RN) has given her extensive insight into the conventional Western approach to health care and see firsthand the negative, systemic effects to our bodies caused by the food industry and big pharma.

Chelsie walked through her own experience of enduring a season of prolonged sickness where everything she knew was challenged and nothing she tried worked. Her physicians focused on and treated her symptoms without addressing the root causes of her illness. This sparked an interest in her to find answers, not just treatment.

Chelsie has a passion for natural healing and wholeness. This passion has driven her to intense research into how the body works, how food is medicine, and how God designed our bodies to heal themselves. Her focus is on wholeness—spirit, soul, and body.

An ordained minister with Joan Hunter Ministries, Chelsie believes in the power of supernatural healing and the importance of stewardship over the body as a resource given by God. She is filled with energy, speaks positive words, and lives in joy! Chelsie coaches others into a lifestyle of prayer, quality nutrition, movement, and exercise to walk in wellness and experience wholeness.

"We are spirit, soul, and body—a whole entity. Wholeness requires health in all these areas. We thrive when we embrace heaven's wholeness!"

CHELSIE WARD

SPIRITUAL | PHYSICAL | SOCIAL | EMOTIONAL

Support for You from Chelsie

MENTAL | INTELLECTUAL | ENVIRONMENTAL

I am committed to helping you step into wholeness. Wherever you find yourself right now, I will use my knowledge and expertise to guide you into making better quality decisions that will bring improvement to your life. Here is my pledge to you:

- I will encourage, support, and believe in you—especially when you do not believe in yourself.

- I will remain passionate about helping you create a life you love.

- I will hold you accountable for what you say you're going to do.

- I will help you try new things, take risks, and get out of your comfort zone—I want you to soar!

- I will help you learn to trust yourself and let go of negative baggage.

- I will welcome your thoughts, fears, feelings, failures, and secret yearnings without judgment.

Change is challenging and rewarding. It would be my privilege to help you through coaching to overcome the obstacles facing you so you can access joy and excitement for life!

WWW.CHELSIEWARD.COM

COACHING OPPORTUNITIES WITH CHELSIE WARD

Wholeness from Heaven for You!

Chelsie equips driven professionals who feel overwhelmed and have lost their energy for unknown reasons toward reclaiming their health and getting their life back so they can make a bigger impact in the world.

Her process focuses on three main things:

- ✓ Figuring out which foods work right for your body so it can function at its potential and give you freedom from cravings and uncertainty in what to eat.

- ✓ Uncovering hidden healing opportunities so we can restore balance to your body, using functional lab tests you can do at home

- ✓ Teaching you how to honor your body's needs so it will honor you back as well as create peace with your past so you can move forward in joy and happiness.

Rebuild a healthy foundation to reach optimal health levels.

After assessing your current health history, Chelsie will help you create a realistic plan to remove inflammatory foods and substances, reduce environmental toxin exposure, work to eradicate stressors, improve sleep habits, and give you the tools you need to live in optimal health.

Who will this program help?

This program is for you if you are ready to invest in your future self. It is for those with

- ✓ ADHD
- ✓ Autoimmunity
- ✓ Chronic fatigue
- ✓ Detoxification needs
- ✓ Diabetes or problems with insulin resistance
- ✓ Digestive disorders/Gastric reflux disease
- ✓ Elevated cholesterol
- ✓ Emotional Eating
- ✓ Fibromyalgia
- ✓ Food allergies/intolerances
- ✓ Food/sugar cravings
- ✓ Hormone imbalance
- ✓ Inflammation and joint pain
- ✓ Overweight/Metabolism issues
- ✓ Stress and anxiety

Programs are customized based on your health and budget needs.

VISIT CHELSIEWARD.COM FOR
CURRENT COACHING PACKAGES.

Did you enjoy this book?

Please help me spread the word about healing and wholeness. If you found this book helpful, would you consider sharing it with a friend? Other ways you can help are by asking your local bookstore to carry this title and ordering extra copies to give as gifts. One of the best ways to assist others in finding this information is by posting a review on amazon.com. Here's how!

1. Go to www.amazon.com.
2. Search for **Healed His Way** by Chelsie Ward.
3. Scroll all the way to the bottom and click on the button, "**Write a Customer Review.**"
4. Rate the book (out of 5 stars) and write your review. (Even if you didn't purchase your copy on Amazon, you can still leave a review, just be sure to tell where you got your copy.)
5. Submit, that's all it takes!

Invite Chelsie to Speak at Your Next Event

Chelsie brings the credibility of a medical professional and avid researcher, combines that with her deep faith in God, her passion for wellness, and a charming, delightful personality to deliver informative, intuitive, and inspiring messages to your event. People who encounter her are motivated and encouraged to embrace new hope and healthy habits to walk in wholeness—spirit, soul, and body!

To connect with Chelsie for speaking or coaching, you can follow her on:

- Facebook: **ChelsieWardWellness**
- Instagram: **@Chelsie_Ward_Wellness**
- Website: **www.chelsieward.com**

Printed in the USA
CPSIA information can be obtained
at www.ICGtesting.com
LVHW011608080823
754676LV00008B/338